Our voices

will be heard

SPEAK UP!

We are Unstoppable

USE YOUR VOICE TO CHANGE THE WORLD

RED SHED

*In loving memory of grandpa, Richard Beale,
and his endless love of books
1930–2018
L.C.*

First published in Great Britain in 2019 by Red Shed,
an imprint of Egmont UK Limited
The Yellow Building, 1 Nicholas Road, London W11 4AN
www.egmont.co.uk

Text copyright © Laura Coryton 2019
Illustrations copyright © Egmont UK Limited 2019

ISBN 978 1 4052 9469 0

A CIP catalogue for this book is available from the British Library.

Stay safe online. Any website addresses listed in this book are correct at the time of going to print.
However, Egmont is not responsible for content hosted by third parties. Please be aware that
online content can be subject to change and websites can contain content that is unsuitable
for children. We advise that all children are supervised when using the internet.

Egmont takes its responsibility to the planet and its inhabitants very seriously.
We aim to use papers from well-managed forests run by responsible suppliers.

Our voices will be heard

SPEAK UP!

We are Unstoppable

USE YOUR VOICE TO CHANGE THE WORLD

LAURA CORYTON

RED SHED

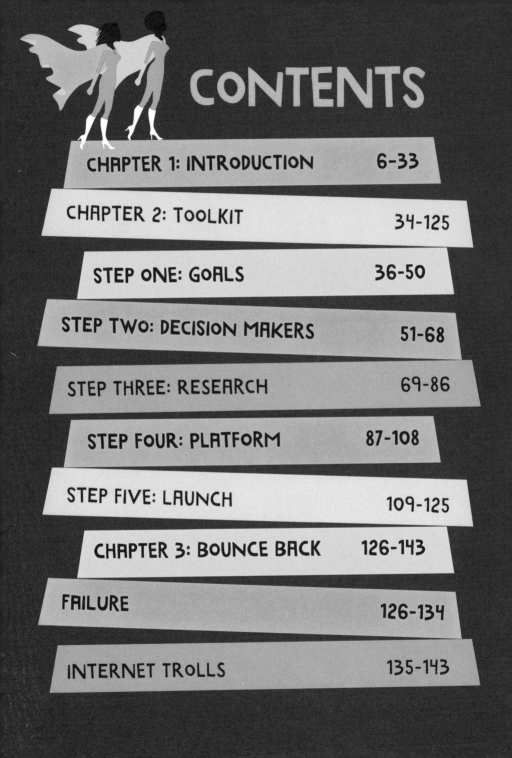

CONTENTS

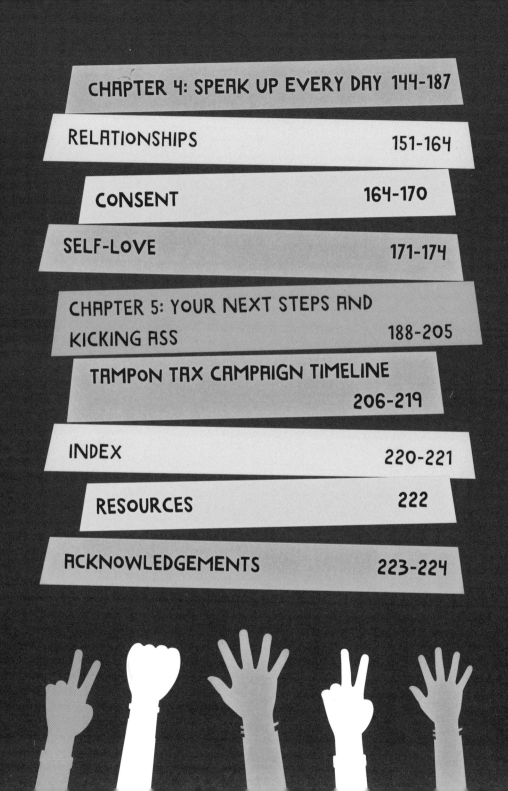

YOU HAVE THE POWER TO CHANGE THE WORLD.
YES, YOU!

IF YOU USE YOUR VOICE, ANYTHING IS POSSIBLE.

This book will help you to change the things in the world that shock you. Or even just annoy you. There is no issue too big or too small that YOU are not able to change. It might take time. It will take a lot of work. But every step we can take to make the world a better place is worth it.

How do I know? I ran a successful campaign that ended the hugely unfair 'tampon tax'. That's right, I said tampon. Don't be shy. I even made the prime minister say the word 'tampon' out loud in Parliament (for the first time in its 800-year history). More on the tampon tax campaign later, but the upshot is: if I can do it, you can too.

There are many issues to feel passionate about. Maybe your local park is being sold off for fancy houses. Maybe your school doesn't offer food for vegans. Maybe you want world peace (don't we all?). Big or small, you can make a difference, but it can be hard to know where to start. So I've written this book to help you change your world.

HOW TO SPEAK UP AND CHANGE THE WORLD!

Before I started my campaign, I had no idea what I was doing. I didn't have training, I don't have any campaigning superpowers or global politician parents to help me. I'm really pretty ordinary. If I can do it, so can you, by using my **FIVE-STEP TOOLKIT** for change.

This book outlines the key steps you need to take to change the world. Together we will get specific about your goals **(STEP ONE)** and get focused on who to target **(STEP TWO)**. I'll show you how to be smart with your research **(STEP THREE)** and get creative with your platforms (you guessed it – **STEP FOUR!**). Finally, **STEP FIVE** will give you the confidence to plan your launch.

I had a lot of success in my campaign, but I also had a lot of knockbacks. I think it's really important to talk about failing and how to **BOUNCE BACK**. It's not easy, but with help I managed it. We'll also cover a very modern and very unpleasant phenomenon: **TROLLS**. In Chapter 3 we'll talk about how you can use trolls to your advantage. Their biases can empower your voice and legitimize your campaign. Never let them knock your campaigning confidence.

I'VE SAID IT BEFORE AND I'LL SAY IT AGAIN: IF I CAN DO IT, IF THEY CAN DO IT, SO CAN YOU!

If you really care about an issue, don't hold back. Make a change. Ask yourself who else will speak up about your issue if you don't.

NOW IS YOUR TIME TO SPEAK UP!

Channel your inner Emma Watson and speak up about what you believe in. Emma launched the HeForShe campaign at the United Nations, and in doing so she changed the face of feminism.

During her speech, Emma questioned her ability to talk about women's rights, asking: is an actress qualified to speak up about this? Yes. I think she absolutely is – because, as she said in her speech, she cares and wants to make things better. And this is what qualifies you to speak up about the things that you care about too.

So, if you're scared about speaking up, you're in great company. You don't have to start by giving a speech to the whole world. You can start small.

BUT ALWAYS TRUST THAT YOU CAN MAKE A DIFFERENCE.

There's a time for big campaigns but there are also many times for tiny, everyday actions that have a huge impact. In Chapter 4 we're going to talk about some difficult things.

RELATIONSHIPS

CONSENT

SELF-LOVE

These are big topics. You can speak up about them on an everyday basis. It's these conversations that change the world. In Chapter 4 we'll talk about how political the personal really is. By sparking conversations with those around you about these topics, you can challenge prejudices and change narratives.

You can use your voice to find power in lots of everyday situations. Catcalling is just one. When I was at school, I experienced catcalling, sadly, like many, many other female students. It shouldn't happen, but it does. It made me feel uncomfortable. It still does. But since then, I've learned how to deal with the men who call out to me and my friends. What are they thinking anyway? That we'd reply? 'What a great chat-up line! Can we make out right now, please?' Come on.

For years I didn't know what to do, so I did nothing, but it doesn't have to be that way.

This book will help you discover the many ways you can find your power by using your voice.

IT WILL SHOW YOU HOW TO BE THE BADASS I KNOW

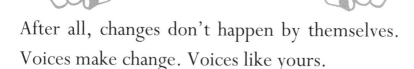

YOU ARE.

After all, changes don't happen by themselves. Voices make change. Voices like yours.

Just like Lucy Gavaghan, teenage animal welfare activist and my inspiring friend (who, in her spare time convinced supermarket giant Tesco to stop selling caged eggs), always tells me:

'Never forget the power a single voice has to make an incredible impact.'

THE INTERNET IS OUR SUPERPOWER!

I never set out to become a campaigner. I didn't dream about ending the tampon tax when I grew up. I'd never even heard of the tampon tax. In fact, our school careers advisor suggested us girls should aspire to careers such as wedding planning, while the boys should aim to be business managers or politicians.

EYE-ROLL!

It wasn't as though I had nothing to speak up against. Believe me, there was plenty I wanted to change! The problem was I never thought I really could change anything.

All I knew was that changing the world sounded pretty far-fetched. What could I, an average person, do anyway? My parents had always reminisced about their generation, which changed the world through rock 'n' roll. In comparison, my friends and I didn't seem too interested in shaking things up, or so I thought . . .

It's confession time: I hate revision. (Surprise!) When I was studying for my university finals that extremely rainy summer I just could not concentrate. I would take any opportunity to be distracted. Luckily my friends felt the same and were posting articles and obscure documentaries all over their social media feeds that happily sent me down an internet rabbit hole for a long time.

And that's when it came to me:

THE INTERNET IS OUR GENERATION'S SUPERPOWER. WE HAVE REDEFINED THE WORLD BY CREATING A NEW ONE ONLINE.

While the internet has enabled us to fill our time with not exactly valuable activities (hello, kitten videos), it has also given us the power to change the world.

OUR GENERATION DOES CARE ABOUT CHANGING THINGS AND SOLVING THE INSTITUTIONAL PROBLEMS THAT WE FACE BECAUSE OF OUR GENDER, RACE, RELIGION AND SEXUALITY.

Just because we're not doing so through the same means as those before us doesn't mean that we aren't already making our own changes in our own, quieter, new ways.

Eventually I ran out of social media updates. I had to start revising. That made me realize something else. (Come with me down this rabbit hole!) Studying had been impossible for millions of women before me. Women had been excluded from university until barely more than a hundred years ago.

When I studied at Oxford I felt this sexism. While men have been studying at the University of Oxford since the 1100s,

IT WAS ONLY IN THE 1920s THAT THE INSTITUTION DEEMED WOMEN WORTHY OF ATTAINING A UNIVERSITY EDUCATION.

Although the institution is making efforts to be progressive, there are many reminders of its past. The dining halls are lined with pictures of professors and alumni to inspire students, but almost all are men.

This got me thinking about politics. Did you know that the word '*democracy*' comes from ancient Greek? The very word combines the words *demos* δῆμος, which means *people* and *kratos* κράτος, which means *force* or *power*. But when democracy was born – in Athens in the 5th century BCE – you had to be a man of a certain age and class to be considered a person or citizen of your city-state. From the birth of democracy, women were excluded from the very concept.

DEMOCRACY?

Political realities today continue to discourage women from engaging in politics. Less than a third of UK MPs are female.

OUT OF THE 193 COUNTRIES THAT ARE MEMBERS OF THE UNITED NATIONS ONLY 16 HAVE A FEMALE HEAD OF GOVERNMENT. THAT'S JUST 9 PER CENT!

Online, the world is different. The world we have created via the internet can be truly democratic. Virtual institutions like the Open University have offered educational opportunities to men and women equally since it was founded in 1969. The internet's political institutions have also smashed gender barriers since they began. Perhaps the most striking example is online petitions.

For years I had signed and shared many petitions and campaigns, and I could see they were super effective! From Lucy-Anne Holmes's **NO MORE PAGE 3** campaign to Laura Bates's **EVERYDAY SEXISM PROJECT**, there was no doubt that women were using the internet to change the world.

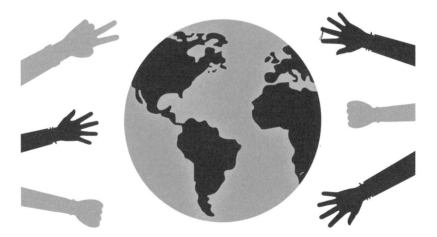

One of the world's leading online petition organizations is **CHANGE.ORG**. They are amazing.

Their UK director, Kajal Odedra tells me that in her experience, women sign, share and support online petitions far more than men do. Women drive change that's instigated and legitimized by online campaigns. As a result, women truly are winning online. Via the internet, women are changing the world. While the majority of online petitions are started by men, more winning petitions are started by and run by women. In many ways we hold the equivalent of political offices and the power to persuade political decision makers through the internet.

That is pretty astounding. It is new. It is exciting. We do not know where it will lead us yet. That is up to us.

Back on that depressingly rainy afternoon, my phone vibrated. I STILL had not started revising . . . so, I looked at my phone and saw my friend Verity had sent me a link to an article.

THIS ARTICLE PRETTY MUCH CHANGED MY LIFE.

It discussed the 5 per cent tax we were paying on period products. At first I presumed this tax must make some sense. If the government backed a tax on period products, then there must be some logic behind it, right? But I wanted to check the logic, so I began to research the UK's taxation system (yes, I really was THAT desperate to avoid revising). This was when things started to get annoying . . . and then shocking. I discovered the extent of the absurdities that riddle our taxation system.

Since 1973, our government deemed products such as tampons and period pads to be luxury items. Yet they aren't plated with gold, nor do they come with a side serving of diamonds. They aren't even an item most of us would want to purchase if we had the choice. Period products are needed by half of the population to engage fully in public life all through the month. It's as simple as that.

While women have paid tax on period products, other more frivolous items have escaped tax altogether. Why? Well, because astonishingly the government appears to have deemed many items more essential than women being able to participate in daily life.

Things such as maintaining private helicopters, eating exotic meats and playing bingo.

Of course, period products are essential to people who menstruate. Yet the government deemed them a 'luxury'. But what makes this story even more astonishing is that the UK was NOT alone in the absurdity of this tax. Oh no. Get this. In Texas, the state government also taxes period products for being 'luxury' products, while they have a zero tax rate for what they deem to be more 'essential' items. Here's the shocking part. Such 'essential' items include

COWBOY BOOTS!

PEOPLE WHO MENSTRUATE WERE BEING TAXED FOR HAVING PERIODS. I WAS SHOCKED. THEN I GOT ANGRY.

Women have been campaigning to end tampon tax for generations. But they haven't always been able to utilize the internet or the new online political world. I was gunning to sign a petition to end the tax, but I couldn't find one.

When I discovered this tax had existed for so long I decided to do something I had never done before.

I STARTED A PETITION.

I didn't think it would be very popular – it was a campaign cocktail of menstruation and taxation after all, not exactly the most thrilling combination of topics!

But I had our generation's superpower to rely on – the internet – and if I didn't try to launch this petition now, who would, and when?

I was shocked again: people did get behind my **END TAMPON TAX** petition. To be more specific, over 320,000 men and women! With this kick-ass cohort of supporters, we got the prime minister to say 'tampon' in parliament and eventually ended this tax in the UK and then in Europe. Not only that, but my initial online petition also spurred women from across the world to start their own End Tampon Tax sister petitions, which are now axing the tax in countries scattered across almost every continent, from India to Australia. Even Michelle and Barack Obama offered their support for the campaign!

That was the beginning of the End Tampon Tax campaign. Since then it has been tackling the period taboo and encouraging women to feel more confident and comfortable in their bodies. Period!

The internet offers a new platform upon which to organize, demonstrate our work and speak up. It's powerful. It makes us distinctly powerful too.

There is power in your voice. There is possibility in the internet. In combining the two, you can change your world.

TIME TO SPEAK UP

So what do you think? I'm guessing if you picked up this book in the first place, you were already interested in some kind of activism. If you picked it up because of the awesome cover (thanks, Elaine!), then I hope this introduction has given you some things to think about.

This book will arm you with the weapons you need to take down the problems you want to tackle. You can read it from beginning to end, using the **SPEAK UP TOOLKIT** as a step-by-step guide to creating your own successful campaign, or you can dip in and out, depending on the kind of advice you're looking for.

Remember, you don't have to launch a global campaign right this second. (You can if you want to, though!) Everyday, small actions can have a big impact. I want you to be confident in your voice, in your views and to give you the tools to make change.

What shocks you in the world? What annoys you? Where do you see injustice that you want to challenge? And who are you to be leading this fight? You are you.

YOU ARE AWESOME.

You are unique. You are powerful and your voice matters. It's time to

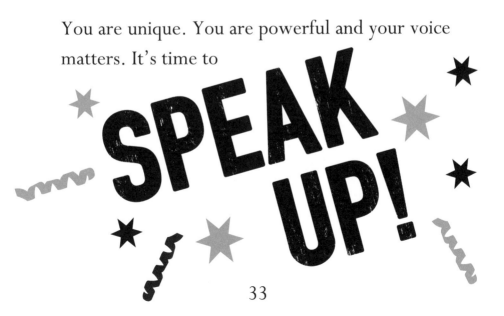

SPEAK UP TOOLKIT

Now you should be all fired up and ready to speak up. But how? I didn't know anything about campaigning when I started, and it can seem like an overwhelming task. Who am I to tell the world to change?

I'M ME. AND YOU'RE YOU.

AND OUR VOICES ARE VALID

AND IMPORTANT.

BUT HOW DO WE GET

OURSELVES HEARD?

Here's where my speak up toolkit comes in! I'm going to share everything I've learned about campaigning with you in this chapter. In my work, I have identified **FIVE STEPS** to get you from having an idea to launching a campaign. We'll cover how to:

1) BE SPECIFIC: IDENTIFY YOUR GOALS

2) BE FOCUSED: FIND YOUR DECISION MAKERS

3) BE SMART: DO YOUR RESEARCH

4) BE CREATIVE: DECIDE ON YOUR PLATFORM

5) BE CONFIDENT: PLAN YOUR LAUNCH

Each section rounds up with handy action tips for activists.

ARE YOU READY?
LET'S GO!

STEP ONE
BE SPECIFIC
GOALS

To launch a killer campaign you must first select a killer, specific campaign goal. This is major. It will form the crux of your campaign. It's important to get it right! Here's how to zoom in on your choice of an issue to tackle:

1) In the most general way possible

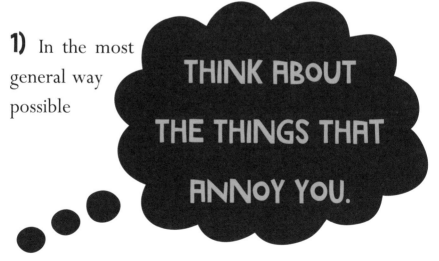

THINK ABOUT THE THINGS THAT ANNOY YOU.

We've got to start by thinking big here. Society is filled with inequality. Depending on who we are and where in the world we are born, some groups of people will have greater advantages and opportunities than others.

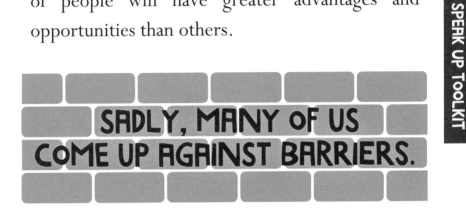

SADLY, MANY OF US COME UP AGAINST BARRIERS.

These barriers vary depending on our race, gender, religion, social class and other things – some are a result of our own life choices, others are just a by-product of who we are and when and where we were born. Sometimes these are called 'institutional problems', meaning that they are a result of how our society has set up institutions like government, schools and industries. And if no one challenges them, these issues just continue.

My End Tampon Tax campaign fell under the institutional problem of sexism. But I didn't realize this at first – not for a long time.

ALL I KNEW WAS THAT I WAS ANNOYED.

I was annoyed at being catcalled on the street. (FYI if a catcaller is reading this, please save the 'Hey, sweet cheeks' for actual legit cats. OK bye.) I was annoyed at the boys at school dominating science, maths and IT while it was presumed I would only like art, food tech and dance. I was annoyed that everyone at school would watch the boys play basketball while nobody supported the sports that us girls played, including Julia (my twin) and me practising taekwondo where we literally kicked ass (FYI Julia earned her black belt and became a pro ninja while I tapped out at green belt – we can't all be ninjas!). I was annoyed!

Initially I thought that I was annoyed at being a girl. But I wasn't.

I WAS CONFUSED BY THE WAYS IN WHICH GIRLS ARE TREATED, AND THAT BOYS WERE TREATED DIFFERENTLY.

Basically I was angry at sexism. That's when I knew I had to change something. I knew I wanted to help tackle the institutional problem of sexism.

BUT WHAT COULD I DO?

This question sat with me for a few years. I knew I couldn't just start a movement calling for sexism to do like a dinosaur and instantaneously become extinct but I wasn't really sure why. For years I was forming these questions unconsciously, challenging the status quo in my mind, and slowly

I LEARNED TO

RECOGNIZE INSTANCES OF

SEXISM IN EVERYDAY LIFE.

WHICH ANNOYED ME.

EVERY. DAY.

Since then I've realized something. Sexism is complicated. It's not a single thing, but rather

a large array of many specific issues. It's the media's hyper-sexualization of women that adds to this concept we call 'sexism'.

IT'S THE PRESUMPTION THAT CEO's WILL BE MALE. IT'S THE MASS SEXUAL HARASSMENT OF WOMEN. IT'S THE SIGNIFICANT PAY GAP THAT SEPARATES THE SEXES.

All of these examples of gender injustices strengthen the wider concept that we call sexism.

This can be applied to racism, ableism, ageism and many other awful-isms, and these are all big, institutional problems, which reveal themselves everywhere from many, many smaller everyday actions and big policy decisions.

IF THIS ANNOYS YOU TOO,

THEN GOOD.

IT SHOULD!

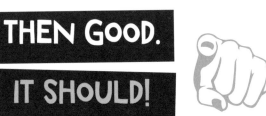

Never stop being shocked and annoyed by the problems that hold people back. But always remember that

YOU HAVE THE POWER

TO CHANGE THEM.

Just like my twin sister always tells me: 'We can do anything.' Try to think about exactly what it is that annoys you, and which institutional problem you might want to tackle through campaigning. Do you want to help reduce racism, sexism or classism? Maybe you want to protect the environment, save animals or support people with disabilities? There are lots of things to be shocked and annoyed by. Choosing just one or maybe a few barriers to tackle can be really difficult. I chose to focus on the problem that I had the most experience of battling – sexism.

This is important to remember. Just like most other institutional problems, thousands of issues constitute sexism throughout almost all societies across the globe. To truly get rid of such problems we need to tackle these more specific issues, one at a time.

2) NARROW YOUR FOCUS:
FIND YOUR SPECIFIC ISSUE

Now we get to the important part: choosing the right issue for you to tackle. This is exciting. This is the moment that you get to choose the focus of your campaign.

While all issues will look different – whether they're examples of sexism or any other institutional problem – all issues that make killer first campaign goals have certain things in common. Above all, they're really specific. While I want to lobby to 'end sexism' (because, wouldn't that be great?), it's too large an issue and too unwieldy to create practical change. There's no silver bullet that can defeat sexism overnight. Sexism is far too vague and large a problem for any one person to bring it down singlehandedly. So we have to break it down.

A specific and effective campaign goal might be to end a particular law or policy that exacerbates sexism or legitimizes sexist views.

THAT'S RIGHT –

THAT'S WHAT MY TAMPON

TAX CAMPAIGN TARGETED!

We were specific about one area of legislation that unfairly taxed menstruating people.

Now, sometimes, there's no pleasing some people. We got asked what good one little campaign goal like tampon tax was when sexism at large still exists. This is frustrating, but you will definitely encounter such people on your campaigning journey, so I want you to be prepared with a kick-ass answer! If someone challenges you like this, for example, they say, 'What use is lobbying to tighten street harassment laws? Why don't you try to ban sexism?'

Try not to roll your eyes. Ask them if they would suggest we stop researching cures for breast cancer, or any individual cancers, because instead we should really be trying to cure death? Chances are, they will agree that such a suggestion would be ridiculous and impossible. Similarly, we can't cure society of sexism without treating the issues that cause it.

I like to think of sexism as if it were a tree. Yes, that's right! If sexism is a tree, then as campaigners, we are mighty tree surgeons! To take down the tree of sexism and get to the roots of the problem (quite literally!) we need to tackle its branches one at a time. Each branch represents a specific example of the wider problem of sexism. Once all of these examples are solved, and we have subsequently hacked at each branch of our sexism tree, then we will be left with nothing but its trunk! The tree would be no more. We would have won!

Whichever wider problem you are helping to solve, whether it's sexism, racism, anti-Semitism or something entirely different, you too are acting like a mighty tree surgeon. You are working towards cutting down your problem as if it were a tree. Each super specific campaign you run will do an amazing job in cutting down a branch of your chosen tree of problems. Soon they will all be taken down to the ground!

Just like campaigning trans activist/author Charlie Craggs says:

'We might not be able to change the world on our own but if we all do our bit to change the world, the world will change.'

Ending tampon tax was a killer first campaign goal/perfect branch for me because it was really specific. Ending tampon tax was about axing a particular tax policy. It was tangible. It was something I could pinpoint and I felt confident that I could help to dislodge it.

What will your first campaign goal be?

YOU CAN CHANGE ANYTHING, ANYWHERE IN THE WORLD.

What are you passionate about? What example of the institutional problem that annoys and shocks you do you want to bring to an end once and for all? There is so much to choose from here. It might be helpful to draw your issue as if it were a tree so that you can see all of its branches. Then you can choose which one to pick first!

Perhaps you might want to change Wimbledon's tennis dress code, which for some bizarre reason currently encourages female tennis players to wear skirts rather than shorts (they're athletes and they play tennis to win, not to be sexualized – am I right?), or maybe you want to lobby for the creation of a legal definition of 'stalking' (yep, that's right, the law deals with stalking so badly that it STILL isn't strictly legally defined). Perhaps your local train station is not accessible for disabled people or maybe your local park is filled with statues of men with no female representation at all and you want to fix these things. Well, you can! Whatever your goal,

ANYTHING IS POSSIBLE

when you put your mind to it. Always remember that you can do anything and that no problem is too big to be tackled by a mighty change-maker and tree surgeon, just like you!

3) WRITE IT DOWN!

I suggest you keep notes throughout this toolkit. Not only will this help you organize your campaign, but it will keep you focused and be an awesome record of all your hard work. If your motivation is ever flagging, you can look back through your notes to see how far you've come!

The goal is your inspiration. The goal is your driving force. Always keep it close to your heart. Never forget what you're aiming for.

You'll find my action tips for activists over the next four steps. Here are your first ones:

ACTION TIPS FOR ACTIVISTS

1. Think big, think broadly, think about the institutional problems that annoy you in the world. Think about which problem you want to help change (e.g. 'sexism')
2. Narrow that down to identify your campaign goal. Make that goal specific, make it tangible (e.g. End Tampon Tax) and . . .
3. Write it down!

STEP TWO
BE FOCUSED
DECISION MAKERS

You've reached our second step to making changes! You're on your way to building your very own campaign, but to make sure you're confident and passionate about your issue there are a few pieces of prep that need to be taken care of first.

It's time to find out who you are targeting. This step is all about identifying who your decision maker(s) are. Your decision maker(s) hold the power to implement the change that you want to see. They are the people, person, organization or governing body that you will need to lobby. They are the ones you ultimately need to persuade to make your change.

51

This may seem pretty straightforward but trust me, it is not always as simple as it sounds. Here's how I discovered who my decision makers were, just to showcase how tricky it can be!

THE TAMPON TAX

DECISION MAKERS:

Once I found my issue of tampon tax I started to wonder who my decision makers were. I figured I would have to try to instigate a national change, but I had no idea how tax worked. Was there some form of national tax lord I should be lobbying?

You won't believe this, but I found there really was a national tax lord that I needed to lobby! This being's official title is the Chancellor of the Exchequer and in 2014 his name was George Osborne. He was my decision maker.

To increase my chances of getting any kind of a response from the chancellor, who is presumably perpetually very busy, I did three things at once: I sent a letter to my local MP asking for his support and advice, I contacted the chancellor directly asking if he would change our taxation policy on period products, and I promoted an online petition via social media to gather as many signatures as possible. This all paid off! I got responses from both my local MP and the chancellor's office (we'll talk about this in Step Three).

Once we hit 10,000 signatures on the petition, politicians started to take notice of us.

The first to contact change.org to support our petition was the amazing Stella Creasy MP, and others soon followed, including the badass Paula Sherriff MP. I was lucky enough to be able to meet with both of these superwomen, who gave us unwavering support and advice throughout the campaign. I still meet with Paula Sherriff today to plot future campaigns! Both of these MPs changed the course of our petition. Their support was invaluable. Similarly, if an MP ever asks to meet with you about your petition, then go for it!

BUT REACHING OUR DECISION MAKER WAS NOT QUITE AS EASY AS THAT. OH NO.

In 2015, I discovered that tampon tax was not just a UK issue. The European Union (EU) influences certain rules in all member states and regulates some taxation across all 28 EU member countries.

In 2015 this included the UK, and it included the tampon tax. My heart broke. For over a year we had been trying to influence the WRONG decision maker! I wondered whether I had let down all of the amazing people who had signed my campaign and believed that together, we could end tampon tax? I worried that I had wasted everyone's time. I felt like a failure.

Then I thought of something my ninja twin had told me. She said that:

'Whenever I felt I had failed I just needed to move in a new direction.'

I soon realized that I needed to embrace this news and follow the new direction we had to move in.

I began to target my new decision maker, the EU. This change in direction boosted our support base. Maybe these new supporters thought that because this was such a weird and complicated issue we needed more support. And they were right, we did! Soon **WE HIT 200,000 SIGNATURES!** This made a HUGE difference. Finally George Osborne announced his support for team End Tampon Tax! He was unable to axe tampon tax in the UK, as we discovered this was actually under the EU's jurisdiction, but that doesn't mean he gave up. Oh no. Instead he did something AMAZING! In his Autumn Statement of 2015, the chancellor launched the Tampon Tax Fund, which has given £15m (the same amount the government earned annually in tampon tax revenue) a year to female-focused charities ever since. This has funded lots of important projects, including a brilliant drive to improve gynae cancer research by charity, The Eve Appeal. It has changed lives.

THAT'S PRETTY KICK-ASS!

Then, something even more BADASS happened.

THE THEN PRIME MINISTER

DECIDED TO SUPPORT US.

No WAY, RIGHT? YES WAY!

HERE'S HOW:

In 2016, the EU referendum was called. The prime minister was under pressure to prove that the EU is progressive and helpful. He must have thought 'What better way to prove this than by ending tampon tax?'. YES, David Cameron, our thoughts exactly! So he went to the EU and proposed a motion to all 28 of its member states. This motion would allow all EU countries to lower their taxes on period products to their lowest national taxation rate, which means 0 per cent for the likes of the UK. It passed with the unanimous support of all member countries.

THIS DAY WAS EPIC!

A few days later, David Cameron made a speech in the House of Commons. He announced the END of tampon tax! Despite all of the many setbacks we faced and complications over finding our decision makers, we had finally WON! For the first time EVER, a UK prime minister uttered the word 'tampon' in Parliament – the unrivalled highlight of my life so far – and we knew we were on the road to success.

What I learned from this was that mistakes aren't always as scary or campaign-shattering as they might appear at first. Much to the contrary, mistakes can be fixed and they might even end up strengthening your campaign. Campaigns evolve. They can change if you find you're lobbying the wrong decision maker.

YOU JUST FIND OUT WHO THE RIGHT DECISION MAKER IS AND GO AFTER THEM. RUN!

That was our (somewhat bumpy) journey to finding our decision makers. To find out who your decision maker is, you'll need to decide what kind of campaign you want to run. There are three buckets that campaigns will generally fall into and each needs a different approach, because each will have different decision makers. These buckets are: political, social and commercial change. Here are a few ideas on how to find your campaign focus:

1) POLITICAL CAMPAIGNS

Political campaigns are badass. They seek changes to policies, laws and technical things like funding. To find out who your political decision makers are you need to ask yourself what level of political change you're seeking: local, national or (let's think big here!) international.

LOCAL

Lots of campaigns that make local things happen benefit entire communities. Local changes are incredibly impactful. They're important. If you're pursuing local changes, such as a change in detention policy within your school or more mental health support for your community, then your decision maker will probably be a local governing organization, like your school governing body or local council. They are the ones who hold the ultimate power to instigate your local change.

NATIONAL

If you're making a campaign that will change a national law or policy (just like my End Tampon Tax campaign), then you will usually lobby the government. More specifically a particular government minister might have the ultimate power to make your change. For example, it was the Chancellor of the Exchequer who technically ended tampon tax for us (after our round-Europe detour!). Try to find the right department for your campaign, whether it's the Department for Education, the Government Equalities Office, the Home Office or an entirely different department, and then target the minister responsible for this area of government.

INTERNATIONAL

Finally, international political campaigns (like those that want to change international laws) tend to change the world on a slightly more removed level. Changing international law often does not directly change people's lives immediately. But it does allow for other campaigns to utilize these changes and influence their national laws which will change lives. Don't be discouraged: if you're hoping to change an international law then you're enabling others to change their lives. You're still doing amazing things.

If you're going to implement international changes, then you'll probably be lobbying an international organization, such as the UN, NATO or the EU. These bodies can be really complicated. However, they will all usually have ministers or individuals that lead departments dedicated to

61

certain changes. For example, I found out that I needed to lobby the European Commissioner for Finance to instigate the tampon-tax-ending change to EU law that secured my campaign's UK victory. Similarly, if you find the department that relates most directly to your campaign then you can identify your decision maker(s) too.

CHAPTER 2

TOP TIP: If you ever worry that you're not capable of making your change, think of my papa's favourite saying: 'if you think you are too small to make a difference, try sleeping in a room with a mosquito.' Speaking from experience of living in mosquito-filled Portugal, it's true!

Political changes don't have to be large. They can be everyday actions. This could include conversations with your friends and family about taboo subjects that really shouldn't be taboo (like periods!), hush-hush topics like mental health and self-harm, or even something entirely different – like countries introducing new laws in support of the LGBTQ+

community, including India, which decriminalized gay sex just last year! Talking about these topics is so important. It spreads awareness of them. It gets people thinking about the problem you're interested in solving.

Even 'liking' pages on Facebook, 'following' a change-maker in your field of interest on Twitter or 'reposting' an article about the problem you're tackling on Instagram makes a big difference. You're spreading your message. You're supporting other tree surgeons/change-makers. Vocal campaigners empower other campaigners. Ripples become waves.

YOUR EVERYDAY
ACTIONS CAN MAKE
A HUGE IMPACT.

2) IMPACTFUL SOCIAL CHANGES

Some campaigns aren't dedicated to changing a particular policy or law. They aren't directed at altering anything tangible. Instead they want to change the ways that we think about something in particular. They are awesome too. For example, some campaigns promote messages of self-love and body positivity (see Chapter 4 for more information!). They want to change the way women in society are viewed and in doing so they hope to

 EMPOWER AMAZING WOMEN LIKE YOU!

If you're hoping to instigate a similar change in mindset, then your decision maker will usually be the general public, or perhaps a particular group of people, such as girls. But you CAN make this tangible. Think specifically about what you want.

For example, if you want to increase body positivity and diversity then you might want to challenge the media's representation of female bodies. You could lobby the editors of a specific women's magazine to put more diverse body shapes/sizes/colours on their covers. Or you could campaign for a specific brand of make-up to include women of all shapes/sizes/colours on their advertisements. The possibilities are endless. You can change anything if you think specific and make sure your change is tangible.

3) SPECIFIC COMMERCIAL ALTERATIONS

Lots of campaigns want to change the way products are packaged or the information that is available on goods. These campaigns can be really impactful if they are specific and work towards clear goals. If you are campaigning to alter an aspect of a commercial product, then the producer of that product will usually be your decision maker.

AWESOME ACTIVIST

Amazing MP Paula Sherriff led a campaign to put breast and gynae cancer awareness information on the side of popular period product packages. Her decision maker was Procter & Gamble, the producer of Always sanitary pads and Tampax tampons. She recently won this campaign and in doing so she's increased awareness of these female-specific cancers.

ASK A LOT OF QUESTIONS

Whatever type of campaign you're preparing to launch, all change-makers can benefit hugely from asking others for advice.

DON'T BE SHY.

If you're hoping to make changes to your school policy, ask your teachers, family and librarians who they think you should be targeting, or who can give you the technical advice that you need.

THE INTERNET ALSO OFFERS THE KEY TO A WHOLE WORLD FULL OF INFORMATION.

IF YOU HAVE ACCESS TO IT,

USE IT.

You may find that you have multiple decision makers, just like the End Tampon Tax campaign, which ended up lobbying both the Chancellor of the Exchequer (nationally) and the EU (internationally) to change their tampon tax policies simultaneously. That is completely fine. Campaigns can lobby more than one decision maker. When we found out that we needed to lobby both the UK and EU governments we directed our petition to both the European Commissioner for Finance and the UK Chancellor of the Exchequer. That worked for us, so it can work for you too!

TOP TIP: If you do find that you need to lobby multiple decision makers, it's a good idea to do so through one streamlined campaign. If you start up multiple campaigns to target each decision maker you have, then you'll risk splitting your support base and losing your campaign's focus and momentum. Be focused and coordinate your efforts!

Even though we had to be flexible and change our plan as we went along, eventually we were able to focus our campaign on the key decision makers and were able to enact effective change. Find yours and you can too!

ACTION TIPS FOR ACTIVISTS

Find your campaign 'bucket' – is it political, social or commercial change you're after?

1. Identify your decision maker(s)
2. Keep checking that you're lobbying the right people!

STEP THREE

BE SMART

RESEARCH

Now you've identified both your campaign goal and your decision maker, you're ready to take your next big step: research.

I like to think of campaigns as if they are marathons. Now I am not exactly a big fan of running and I'm certainly not keen on any form of competitive running – or 'racing' as some people might prefer to call it – and you don't have to be either, but campaign races are something entirely different.

Your supporters (aka amazing petition signers) will cheer you on and motivate you throughout your race, while reporters will help you to raise awareness of your journey. This will be exciting! But remember not to get too distracted. Marathons are pretty long! They are difficult. But no challenge is too great for a change-maker like you. Always keep your eyes on the prize: your finishing line (aka your campaign goal).

ONCE YOUR CHANGE IS IMPLEMENTED, YOU WILL HAVE FINISHED YOUR RACE. YOU'LL HAVE WON!

You won't be alone. Just like in the London Marathon, there will be a whole host of others on this race with you. They just don't know where or what the finishing line is yet. And it's your job to point them towards it! Imagine your decision maker standing beside you at the starting line.

YOUR JOB IS TO RUN OUT AHEAD OF YOUR DECISION MAKER

and point out exactly what they will need to do to finish your race and implement your change ASAP. (It is a race after all – time is of the essence!)

HOW DO WE DO THIS?

We plan the race route. You need to research the terrain from your starting line to your finishing line, then plan the best way to get everyone there. From mountaineering the highest piles of legislation to battling through forests of reporters, it may well be challenging. But if you do your research, you'll soon be prepared for anything.

That's why the research you do at this early stage will be utterly invaluable to you in your campaign quest. Planning is major. It is key to overcoming any obstacles you'll face. Every single one. If you can plan your route through your campaign race now, and discover what you need to do to succeed before you even step one foot on your racetrack, you'll be in a stronger position to win.

SIDE NOTE:

Our sister tampon tax campaigners in Canada spent SIX MONTHS planning their campaign route to success before they even launched their petition. When they decided to launch their campaign, they ended tampon tax within THREE months.

★ ★ BOOM. ★ ★

It just goes to show, research is super important!

To plan your campaign route effectively you need to ask yourself three questions:

1) WHAT IS YOUR STORY?

2) HOW WILL YOUR DECISION MAKER IMPLEMENT YOUR CHANGE?

3) WHAT ARE THE STEPS ALONG YOUR ROUTE TO THE FINISHING LINE?

We'll look at the End Tampon Tax roadmap soon, but first I want to share the stories of our sister school projects and how they answer these three questions.

These projects campaign to provide free period products in school toilets in the UK. Here's how and why . . .

1) WHAT IS YOUR STORY?

A campaign's story is so important. This story will demonstrate why your change needs to happen, what motivates you and what puts the 'kick-ass' into your change.

It will persuade a whole heap of people to support you and may well win your campaign.

Kajal Odedra, UK director of leading online petition site change.org, explains the importance of a campaign's story:

'Storytelling is such a key ingredient to an engaging campaign. Statistics don't get people on board. From your supporters, to decision makers, to journalists, it's the story that is important. Women are amazing at telling these stories.'

We launched our sister school projects after an amazing charity called Freedom4Girls found that a staggering 10 per cent of schoolgirls in Leeds miss school because they do not have adequate access to period products. We turned that statistic into a story by explaining that: period poverty is affecting the education of girls. That is not OK. Showing the school governing body (aka the decision makers) that providing free period products in school toilets will help girls to stay in school is a persuasive story. It also simultaneously tackles the period taboo one tampon at a time.

★ ★ BOOM ★ ★

YOUR TURN

It's time to write down some of your ideas about your campaign's story. What will persuade people and your decision makers to back YOU? How do you get from statistic to story?

2) HOW WILL YOUR DECISION MAKER IMPLEMENT YOUR CHANGE?

To lobby your decision makers effectively you will need to know what you want them to do, and how. To ensure your campaign wins ASAP you will need to make it as easy as possible for them to enact the change you want! You don't need to be an expert in the field of your campaign.

WHAT YOU NEED TO DO IS
PROVE YOUR GOAL IS POSSIBLE.

This will strengthen your power to persuade and ultimately to win.

Many of the schoolgirls who lead our school project campaigns do not initially know how to change school policy.

That too is completely OK. What is important is to

SPEAK UP
AND ASK FOR ADVICE.

Our girls asked their teachers, librarians, family and friends how to go about their specific campaigns. Each school will implement changes slightly differently. We were able to help them with information on how period products might be made available: schools can decide to allocate funds to it, and they can put in a practical plan about who is in charge of ordering products and distributing them.

Armed with their research, the schoolgirls were able to state clearly what they wanted (free period products), when (ASAP), and how the decision makers could make it happen (deciding to allocate school budget to this cost). They created a persuasive and powerful campaign message.

YOUR TURN

Think about how your decision maker(s) can enact the change that you want to see. It's OK if you don't have all of the answers. Focus on how you can prove that your change is possible, and you can win! If you can find a precedent, you can show your decision maker how easy it is to make a change. If there's no precedent, they can still be the first to make the change! Someone has to be first, and it's ALWAYS OK to ask for help!

3) WHAT ARE THE STEPS TO THE FINISHING LINE?

It's time to plan out the steps that YOU need to take in order to secure your campaign's success. Your steps could be small or big, cautious or ambitious. Channel your inner Jane Fonda, world-class actress, who I think encourages people to learn as much as possible in order to speak up and change the things that matter most.

Jane campaigned against the Vietnam War in America

in the 1970s. It was a very divisive issue and she was extremely brave in speaking out. Plus, she's still acting in top movies today, in her seventies. We need more Hollywood badass women like her! These steps will ensure you know all you can, so that you can speak up as loud as possible and make your change!

Our sister projects instigate school-based changes, so actions typically revolve around school governing bodies. Each project is different, but their typical steps are:

1. **Generate as much school-based support as possible. This might involve creating petitions signed by both teachers and students. Writing school newspaper pieces, speaking on your school radio and raising the issue with school councils also strengthens support.**

2. **Present all of this hard work to the head teacher or governing body of the school and propose the change.**

3. **The governing board or head will agree and implement the change (whoop whoop!).**

TOP TIP: All campaigns face trials and tribulations. Groundbreaking TV producer Shonda Rhimes has talked about how important it is to focus not on our problems but on how we can overcome them. Don't let anything hold you back. Plan your steps optimistically. Block out of your mind whatever might go wrong and keep in mind that anything is possible!

YOUR TURN

Think about the steps that you need to take to make sure your change happens. You may think of lots of steps, or very few! You don't have to limit yourself to the steps you set out at this early stage, but plotting your route through your unknown campaigning race course will help you to cross your finishing line and make your change happen as soon as humanly possible.

Whether your steps turn out perfectly or not, always keep going. You can get to the finishing line even if you have to amend your route mid-race just like we did many, many times!

Here's how we tackled the three killer
questions of research:

OUR STORY

The story that fuelled and won my tampon tax
campaign was the strange way our tax system
worked. While HMRC appeared to prioritize
items such as bingo, which escapes tax altogether,

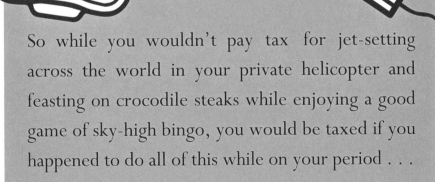

IT DEEMED PERIOD PRODUCTS LUXURIOUS ENOUGH TO BE TAXED.

So while you wouldn't pay tax for jet-setting
across the world in your private helicopter and
feasting on crocodile steaks while enjoying a good
game of sky-high bingo, you would be taxed if you
happened to do all of this while on your period . . .

MAKE SENSE?

WE DIDN'T THINK SO EITHER.

It was this blatantly unfair story that won us huge support. When people asked 'Why does tampon tax matter?' we could say that it TOTALLY mattered because our tax system told girls that consuming crocodile meat was more essential to society than their full engagement in public life. We were able to say this because we did the research. We found our 'story'.

HOW DID OUR DECISION MAKER MAKE CHANGE?

Ending tampon tax meant legally changing national taxation policy. That's a pretty technical issue that I had absolutely no knowledge of. But that was OK. It is really important to remember that you do not have to be an expert to shake things up. Never let that stop you from starting a campaign.

I found out that tampon tax had been lowered from 17.5 per cent to 5 per cent in 2001. That was my precedent and enough evidence to prove more could be done to abolish it entirely. That's all the expert knowledge I needed to go ahead and campaign with!

THE STEPS ALONG OUR ROUTE, FROM START TO FINISH:

This change was a political one, so our actions revolved around Parliament. These were our steps:

CREATE A PETITION:

We got over 10,000 signatures on our petition, the amount you need to gain the attention of Parliament.

PRESENT PETITION TO LOCAL MP:

MP DAWN PRIMAROLO RAISED THE ISSUE IN PARLIAMENT:

EARLY DAY MOTION (EDM): ✓

EDMs are essentially a declaration. They declare that Parliament has an interest in a certain topic or issue. Our first tampon tax EDM proved that Parliament was taking our issue seriously. They were listening to our campaign. They declared their interest in ending tampon tax, period! It was signed by 70 out of 650 MPs, which is way more than we ever expected! (Usually they only get about 10.)

LOBBY DECISION MAKER: ✓

We handed our petition to Number 11 Downing Street to ask for chancellor George Osborne's support.

PARLIAMENTARY VOTE ON THE ABOLITION OF TAMPON TAX: ✗

BUT WAIT! Sadly, this vote was unsuccessful. (More of this in Chapter 3 on dealing with failures – we had our fair share!) Nonetheless, Parliament later backed our campaign when the EU referendum was announced. Remember: setbacks are OK! Setbacks are to be expected.

WE DID NOT GIVE UP!

LOBBY THE EU: ✔️

David Cameron took our campaign to the EU. Later, I spoke to the European parliament on the importance of axing tampon tax.

IT WAS EPIC!

EU PARLIAMENTARY VOTE ON ENDING TAMPON TAX: ✔️

In an unprecedented vote, the EU decided to allow all member states to reduce their tax on period products to their lowest national rate. This piece of legislation won't come into effect until 2022 (annoyingly these things take a LOT of time) but at least we've got the EU to commit to a deadline, which is major!

WE WON

We got from the starting
line to the finishing line.
We had to revise the route along
the way, we had plenty of setbacks,
but we never gave up, and we
always learned from failures.
You can too.

ACTION TIPS FOR ACTIVISTS

1. Write your 'story'
2. Give your decision makers an easy
   how-to (how can they possibly say no?)
3. Plot your own campaign road map – what
   are the steps you need to hit along the way?
   What are your interim goals
   en route to the finishing line?

STEP FOUR
BE CREATIVE
PLATFORM

OK, you've got your campaign goal, you've identified your decision makers and you've got a campaign road map. It's nearly time to start the race, but not quite! Before you set off you need to get creative and plan the 'how' of your campaign.

World-changing activist Leymah Gbowee said: 'You can never leave footprints that last if you are always walking on tiptoe.' Now, we've talked about the campaign being like a running race. And you definitely want to leave footprints, not tiptoe marks, in your campaign.

87

But – if you let me extend my analogy here! – there are all kinds of races. There are boat races, horse races and car races . . . Let's ramp this up another gear and start talking about what tyre tracks you're going to make in your full-throttle campaign!

If you think of your campaign as a rally race then this step is about choosing the right car(s) with which to win. Here are just a few of the shiny four-wheeled vehicles you can use to make sure your campaign is a success:

OPTION ONE
THE OFF-ROAD JEEP, AKA THE PETITION

Your first option is a reliable and lovable off-road jeep. It's a durable vehicle that will happily conquer all kinds of terrain and take you across the world as your loyal sidekick!

Just like a jeep, the petition is a reliable and trusted vehicle for campaigning. Petitions are great.

They can help almost every campaign on the planet. Why? Because they utilize our superpower: the internet! As Kajal Odedra, UK director of change.org, always tells me:

'The internet is one of the most powerful ways of amplifying your voice.'

ONLINE PETITIONS GALVANIZE THIS POWER.

Petitions are impactful for two reasons. Firstly they clearly demonstrate the number of people that support you. With an online petition these people might come from anywhere in the world – from London to Sydney – because the internet is borderless. By spreading campaign messages across the World Wide Web, petitions can generate vast numbers of signatures. It's this huge quantity that in turn generates power.

IT'S MUCH HARDER TO IGNORE A PETITION THAT GAINS HUNDREDS OR THOUSANDS OF SIGNATURES!

Secondly, online petitions kick ass because they offer all campaigners a fabulous and centralized tool for organization. Once an amazing supporter signs your petition, they also give you their:

1. EMAIL ADDRESS
2. INTEREST
3. TIME

These things are so valuable. Treasure them. You can email your support base to help you at any time. They will ensure you make your change together.

DOES THIS ALL SOUND TOO GOOD TO BE TRUE?

WELL, IT'S NOT!

BUT jeeps aren't always the most fuel-efficient cars. Sometimes, neither are petitions. It takes a lot of time and energy to keep the momentum of a petition going. Not all petitions attract hundreds of signatures immediately – it can take a lot of work to get yours noticed by supporters. And once an amazing supporter does sign your petition you will need to keep them updated with your campaign's progress to make sure they remain interested and invested in your change. Therefore you will need to keep making steady progress. Make sure it's right for you before you start one.

Petitions are best if you're campaigning on one focused campaign goal.

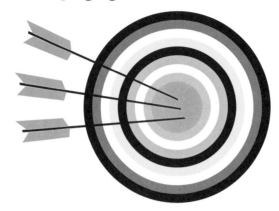

They're effective when it's beneficial to prove that a vast number of people support you no matter where they're from in the world. If you're hoping to change a series of things, or your campaign is specific to your local area, then perhaps a jeep, or a petition, isn't the right vehicle for you.

For example, if you want to instigate a change within your school, then presenting an online petition to your school governing body signed by thousands of people who have no connection to your school whatsoever, might not be too persuasive. But what about a mini-jeep?

Because, on the other hand, producing an offline petition signed by hundreds of students, teachers and parents of those actually attending your school might be much more powerful.

Think a jeep (or mini-jeep) or a petition approach might not be for you? No sweat! You have plenty of other options to choose from.

OPTION TWO
THE TANK, AKA THE LETTER

Tanks are hefty vehicles.

They mean some serious business. They may not be the fastest option and they certainly won't get you to the finishing line in a matter of seconds, but they will endure all kinds of terrain – even more so than our trusted jeep – and can make impressive blows in the process. While tanks aren't usually a racing driver's number-one choice of vehicle, they might just be perfect to help you win your race.

Letters are amazing. You can compose a fierce and persuasive letter to anyone you wish, asking for practically anything you like! They are a straightforward way to ask for information you need, like support, advice or even collaboration!

WHO DO YOU SEND

YOUR LETTERS TO?

So who might you consider contacting, and what for? Well, this could be anyone connected to your change. The possibilities are endless! I contacted countless people and organizations to ask if they supported/had advice for/could collaborate with my End Tampon Tax campaign. Each person/

organization/group that gave me their support strengthened my campaign and legitimized my argument. If they supported me and the goal of my campaign then why shouldn't our decision maker, George Osborne MP?

Think about who you can contact to strengthen your campaign, besides the decision makers you are targeting.

HOW TO CONTACT ORGANIZATIONS

Brands can sometimes give your campaign a triumph if you write to them. Contacting them may even spark the creation of new campaigns run by these organizations, inspired by yours! For example, Bodyform who produce period pads have donated tens of thousands of packs of their products to homeless shelters and women's charities tackling period poverty, in response to our campaigns. That is pretty cool!

Never be afraid to ask for the help of big brand names. You never know what might come from it! You can find the email addresses and names of those to contact within big brands on their websites. Or go direct to their social media feeds!

DON'T FORGET POLITICIANS!

Even if they're not your direct decision maker, politicians are influential. They can help you make your change happen. Think big here. Don't just contact UK politicians. Those further afield might also be persuasive heavyweights to have on your side! For example, foreign politicians might be super helpful. If they support you, then they prove there is international pressure for your change to finally be made.

THAT'S PRETTY PERSUASIVE!

YouTuber Ingrid Nilsen got the chance to interview Barack Obama for AJ+ about a whole load of issues back in 2016. At that time, our sisters in the USA (led by superwoman, Jennifer Weiss-Wolf) had begun to make waves in ending the tampon tax, stateside. They sent the YouTube star letters to ask if she would ask Barack Obama about tampon tax. She did not disappoint. Ingrid Nilsen AMAZINGLY did just that. How did Obama respond? Well, he gave the coolest and slickest answer IN HISTORY. (He is SO cool.) The former president said that he had 'no idea' why tampon tax was a thing. Well, Obama, neither do we! Even more amazingly, he then said he thought it might be because the laws had been made by men. *heart eyes*

97

He became the first world leader to connect tampon tax with female political underrepresentation. If we don't have women in politics, then issues affecting women won't be fairly debated, governed or solved. Half of the population will be left behind. Tampon tax demonstrates this. Barack Obama says so, so it must be true. (Am I right?)

Oh, and he concluded by saying that Michelle Obama would agree that tampon tax should be axed.

BEST. POWER. COUPLE. EVER.

It just goes to show how important sending letters can be, even to the other side of the pond!

TOP TIP: You can find the contact details of all local and national politicians at *www.writetothem.com*

What might your tank look like? Well, there are many ways to phrase a killer letter, but here is one relatively informal example that might help to kickstart your ideas:

Dear _____ ,

I am writing to ask if you would kindly offer your support for my campaign to [insert your kick-ass change]. Having started this campaign in [insert start date] we have gathered the support of over [insert number of people who support your campaign] and would be delighted if you would join us. With your help we can instigate this change. We very much look forward to your response.

Yours sincerely,

There are a few warnings that come along with choosing the tank, aka the original and mighty letter. First, tanks are quite old-fashioned. Similarly, letters can seem outdated. Campaigners rarely consider their work well and truly done after writing a single letter. If changes really were that easy to make, they probably would have been made already. Secondly, letters can be ignored.

THE PERSON YOU WRITE TO SIMPLY MIGHT NOT WRITE BACK!

They might not be armed with a tank mighty enough to square up to yours. They might not have a reply good enough to send to you.

THAT CAN BE SERIOUSLY FRUSTRATING.

But there are ways to overcome these potential tank-related setbacks.

My advice would be to use your tank, or letter (or both if you actually have a real-life tank) as one of your fleet of campaign-race vehicles. You can use tanks and letters to strengthen any other mode of transport you choose. A jeep doesn't have the ability to blast its enemies. Tanks do. Petitions cannot always make instant impacts. Letters can. Especially when they support shiny friendly jeeps . . . oh, and popular petitions too!

OPTION THREE
THE LAMBORGHINI AVENTADOR, AKA THE DEMO

Lamborghinis are ridiculously awesome cars. They look great. They sound amazing. They make a seriously loud statement. This particular Lamborghini has impressive horsepower (544kW if you must know!), can travel a whopping

350km/h and comes in a variety of colours. Lamborghinis are like demonstrations in SO many ways.

DEMOS ARE ALSO RIDICULOUSLY AWESOME.

They are so much fun, they look great and make a loud, fearless and truly unapologetic statement. Demos excite supporters and gain attention from almost everyone: supporters, politicians and decision makers alike.

Having said that, many words of warning come with the flashy Lamborghini. It is an over-the-top car. Sometimes demos can border on OTT too. That can be good, but it can also harm your campaign in certain ways. By choosing the Lambo you risk the possibility of alienating your support base. For example, turning up to a school in a £270,000 sports car might not be suitable, particularly if you're under the legal age to even pass your driver's test!

Similarly, if you're trying to enact a school-based change, then organizing a demo outside the teachers' staff room as a first step might jeopardize your support. Be careful and sensitive of your supporters. Protesting could harm your credibility and make your change less likely to happen if organized thoughtlessly. Build up to it. You don't want to launch your Lambo-sit-in outside the staff room just to have the teachers say they had no idea pupils felt so strongly about whatever your entirely reasonable request is. They would have said yes immediately, but now you've made a huge fuss and created an 'us and them' atmosphere where there didn't need to be one.

There is one last caution to mention: sports cars are fast cars. To safely and effectively optimize the Lambo's 350km/h potential, you need one crucial thing: a relatively large racecourse. Similarly for a protest to work well and effectively, you need people behind you.

With lots of people behind you and your campaign you will ROCK the racecourse, but if you organize a protest too early it might not be as spectacular as you expected.

TOP TIP: Never be afraid to fail. I have organized a few protests that consisted of myself, my twin and three friends. That was it!! But I've also organized protests that consisted of hundreds of supporters. You won't get it right every time, even with experience or race-car training, so don't let a small protest put you off organizing more in the future.

OPTION FOUR
THE ELECTRIC
BMW i8 COUPE, AKA SOCIAL MEDIA

This electric BMW is unlike anything we've mentioned so far, be that cars, tanks or even my ninja twin! It is undoubtedly the future of racing. Its electric motor makes it environmentally friendly and cost effective, while its impressive engine gives it the capacity to take you 250km/h and goes from 0 to 100km/h in 4.4 seconds. It's truly awesome!

The Coupe is a thing of the future and so is social media. Like the Coupe, social media has the capability to take your campaign from nought to thousands of supporters in a matter of hours, if not minutes, when you use it correctly. Simply creating a Twitter account for my End Tampon Tax petition

DOUBLED
ITS SIGNATURES OVERNIGHT!

The electric BMW promotes green energy and proves that an electric vehicle is just as awesome as any other. It has an environmental message.

SOCIAL MEDIA CAN ALSO

BE USED TO PROMOTE

MESSAGES CHAMPIONED

BY YOUR CAMPAIGN.

If you're lucky enough to have access to a Coupe, you would probably drive it. Spinning around town in a shiny BMW is a pretty tantalizing temptation to resist! Well, similarly, if you're lucky enough to have access to the internet, you should use it too!

I know this doesn't apply to everyone. Only 90 per cent of the UK currently has internet coverage. When I lived in rural Devon I had to go to the centre of a graveyard on top of a sheep-covered steep hill to access the one bar of mobile signal that graced the town. No joke. But if you live in an area with great internet connection, then don't be shy about using it! Social media gives you access to the most influential people on the planet! That's pretty amazing. Make sure you use these opportunities.

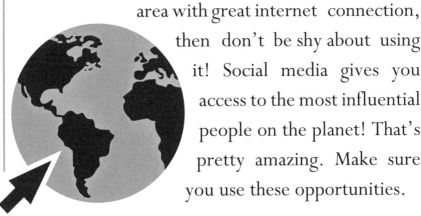

Social media can be used both alone and in support of other campaigning platforms. Imagine racing in both this flashy BMW AND A TANK? Well, you can! For example, Instagram is an amazing photo-sharing social media platform. SO many people run countless campaigns through the app! These incredibly varied Instagram accounts raise awareness of things like body positivity, feminist debates and mental health. They inspire other people to start similar accounts and in doing so they spread similar messages. And just as effective are campaigns that start offline and then use Instagram to promote their change.

Feel free to use, or not use, as many aspects of the internet and social media as you feel comfortable with. We'll talk about some of the darker sides to social media in Chapter 3. But, most importantly, remember: YOU are in control of the internet, not the other way round.

ACTION TIPS FOR ACTIVISTS

Identify your racing-car platform portfolio to what suits your campaign:

1. Petitions
2. Letter
3. Demonstration/protest
4. Social media aka online activism

STEP FIVE

BE CONFIDENT

LAUNCH

Congratulations, you've reached the fifth and final golden step to making kick-ass changes! You are almost ready to graduate from campaigning boot camp.

HOORAY!

So far you've climbed four epic steps:

1) BE SPECIFIC: IDENTIFY YOUR GOALS

2) BE FOCUSED: FIND YOUR DECISION MAKERS

3) BE SMART: DO YOUR RESEARCH

4) BE CREATIVE: DECIDE ON YOUR PLATFORM

Now we need to talk about how you are going to launch your campaign in a way that maximizes all of the hard work you have already done to get to this point.

TOP PETITION TIP: from UK director of change.org Kajal Odedra: *'There are three main factors in women's online campaigning success: Women are very persistent, they are great storytellers and they are connected to their communities.'* Use these three aspects to take on the world.

Launching your campaign is all about winning supporters. But how will you start?

HOW WILL YOU WIN YOUR VERY FIRST SUPPORTER?

Well, I have to tell you something. People can be strange sometimes. They are more likely to support a campaign backed by lots of people (and therefore probably in need of fewer further supporters) than to back a new campaign with fewer supporters (and therefore probably in need of more). If a stranger sees a campaign that is well liked, they will presume it is a legitimate campaign and that backing it is a reasonable thing to do, since lots of people back it and 'lots of people' seem unlikely to be entirely wrong.

Similarly, it might be intimidating for someone who doesn't know you to be the very first person to sign your jeep (aka petition), get behind your tank (aka letter), jump into your Lambo (aka demo) or 'like' your BMW (aka social media posts). This hesitancy can make starting a campaign quite tricky.

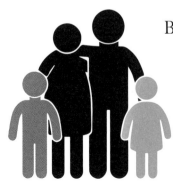

But do not fear! Remember how many people are there to help and support you. They are golden. Do not be afraid to rally your friends, family,

family of friends, aunties, uncles and the cute cat down the street! Don't be shy: ask them all for their support. If you choose to launch a petition, get everyone you know to sign it.

ONCE THEY SIGN IT OTHERS WILL FOLLOW.

SOON YOU WILL BE UNSTOPPABLE!

Launching the End Tampon Tax campaign consisted of me sending my petition to a few of my friends on Facebook just to see what they thought of it. Much to my surprise they posted the petition to their Facebook walls. Suddenly friends of my friends were signing and sharing the petition too, and I didn't even know them! Eventually I went to sleep (which was tricky given all of this excitement) and woke up the following morning with nearly 500 signatures! It was magic and just proves what a little help from your friends and our superpower the internet can do.

TOP TIP: Helen Pankhurst, great granddaughter of suffragette leader Emmeline Pankhurst, author and women's rights activist said: *'I am most impressed by campaigns that are part of a wider story, making the link from the individual or local to the global. My favourites combine fun and purpose. And we should take courage from the suffragettes – from their determination and persistence. I hope generations to come can harness power from their courage.'*

Keep in mind that you do not have to organize a big launch in order to secure a successful campaign. You do not need lots of money (or any money, in fact), experience or volunteers to successfully launch your campaign. You can launch your campaign in lots of ways! You can simply post it on Facebook (like I did) or you can have a bit more fun. You can launch your campaign by creating a video/montage that could convey your campaign

113

succinctly (plus if your video involves cats I'm pretty sure you're guaranteed to triple your signatures). Or maybe an animation might work best for you? Anything visual to accompany your campaign could draw in your audience and make for a successful launch!

Here's what you can expect from the day you launch your kick-ass campaign to every day after that:

DAY 1

The day you press 'publish' on your petition page, you send your letter, you grasp your speakerphone to kickstart your demo, click 'live' on your social media account or any combination of the above, is the day you LAUNCH your campaign! This is the day the fun begins. It's the start of your campaign race.

Everyone's first campaign day is different. Even if two campaigns are lobbying for the same change, they can still have polar opposite launching experiences. For example, my launch day consisted of me clicking 'publish' on my change.org petition page while in my reindeer onesie desperately trying to avoid revising.

On the other hand, our sisters in Canada had planned their launch.

THEY HAD MANY MORE

TRICKS UP THEIR SLEEVE.

As a result their campaign was truly magic! Day one for the Canadian End Tampon Tax team consisted of publishing not only their petition but all of their research, interviews with politicians and info graphs as well. Theirs was a truly smooth and professional operation. Whether you want to launch your petition professionally or like me, you can achieve great results either way.

EVERY DAY AFTER THAT!

With the idea of you as an unstoppable racing driver in mind, let's discuss what to expect after you launch your campaign. Confidence in your ideas, research and a very strong ability to climb up our five steps to making kick-ass changes pretty much has to last forever.

ALWAYS BELIEVE IN YOURSELF AND YOUR WORK.

Here are my top tips to staying positive and sustaining a winning campaign momentum:

Primarily, keeping people interested in your campaign is all about ensuring YOU stay interested in your campaign. So long as you are actively interested and working towards heroically crossing your finishing line, you will do amazing things. Just remember to update supporters with the progress you will already naturally be making by virtue of lobbying for your change. By updating your supporters you are giving them a reason to care and remain interested in your progress. Tell them why they should believe in YOU as their rep for making this change happen. Plus, you get to put a smile on their face when they realize something that they have supported has actually made a difference and that therefore they have made the difference.

YOU WOULD BE NOWHERE WITHOUT YOUR AMAZING, HAPPY, BRILLIANT, PERFECT SUPPORTERS – THEY TOO ARE GOLD!

Loving your campaign is always good. However, remaining interested in your change doesn't always equate to a flawless campaign that enjoys an endless fix of steady progression. That's OK! Because there is another thing that unites campaigns; they all progress in unpredictable ways.

CAMPAIGNS TEND TO DEVELOP SPORADICALLY. CHANGE RARELY HAPPENS STEADILY. SO NEVER BE DISHEARTENED IF YOU HAPPEN TO REACH A CAMPAIGNING LULL.

Get a surfer's mindset: you see, running a campaign is just like surfing in England. Yes, that's right, surfing! In England, weather is a problem. It hails, rains, floods and produces unexpected rainstorms, heatwaves and snowstorms all in practically the same day!

This may be irritating for the average person, but it is particularly annoying for surfers. You can't go out into the ocean if you cannot see the sea through thick mist or hail, snow or rain. Equally you can't surf if the water is too calm and waves do not exist. Mastering the art of surfing is all about accepting the bad weather when it comes and keeping in mind that next time the weather will probably be much better and a good surf is worth the wait.

IT IS ABOUT BEING PATIENT AND ACCEPTING THE THINGS THAT YOU CANNOT CONTROL.

A lot of this is applicable to campaigning. England may have unpredictable weather, but the entire world is pretty unpredictable for campaigners.

You may think you know what is going to happen, just like my weather app tries to foresee the sunshine, but you can never really be sure.

Being able to surf 365 days a year is unlikely given the unpredictability of the weather. Being able to conquer the world of campaigning every day of the year is just as unlikely, but that doesn't mean you cannot ultimately succeed in making your change. People can sometimes be a bit strange. They do not usually accept real change instantly, even if, to you, it is obviously the right thing to do and the change would clearly improve lives.

IT TAKES WORK FROM AMAZING PEOPLE LIKE YOU TO MAKE CHANGE HAPPEN.

OPEN YOUR UMBRELLA.

I know, I know, I'm English and typically obsessed with the weather. But this is a different type of umbrella ...

The type of umbrella that might be useful for the growth of your campaign is the umbrella organizations and charities that could potentially support you and who you could support too.

PARTNERING WITH CHARITIES AND NOT-FOR-PROFIT ORGANIZATIONS THAT TACKLE THE SAME ISSUES AS YOUR CAMPAIGN CAN BE REALLY HELPFUL.

First they can demonstrate that your work has wider implications and secondly it means you get to help an organization that is geared to tackling the same problems as you. For example, the End Tampon Tax petition is partnered with some inspiring charities, including the amazing Eve Appeal that researches and raises awareness of the five gynaecological cancers. We also share a common goal: to fight the taboos and stigmas that hold women back.

The Eve Appeal's CEO Athena Lamnisos wants to tell you that the key to lots of campaigns against stigmas that affect women are:

'Girls and women of all ages breaking culture on tabooed issues. That means straight-talking, proper language and lots of information. You're never too young to call a vagina, well a VAGINA.'

I COULDN'T HAVE SAID IT BETTER MYSELF!

Charities aren't the only organizations that you can partner with. You might also want to think about encouraging others to start new sister campaigns that you can work alongside. There are now End

Tampon Tax sister petitions making changes and ending tampon tax all over the world, from India to the USA! The more sister campaigns that support you, the more obvious it becomes that your change really does need to happen.

ACTION TIPS FOR ACTIVISTS

1. Plan your campaign for day one – and every day after that!
2. Get resilient, with a surfer's mindset
3. Spread the love to other organizations and campaigns under your umbrella.

GRADUATION

That is it! You have completed your speak up crash course on campaigning. You are a fully qualified campaigner ready to take on the world!

You're ready to speak up and begin to make some killer changes.

Feel free to come back to any of the five steps whenever you need to. You might want to refresh your ideas or just remind yourself that you can do amazing things. Because you can! You have walked to the top of our long golden staircase and that is proof in itself of your capabilities.

CONGRATULATIONS!

All that is left for you to do now is to speak up! Just like Emma Rundle, one of my best friends, always tells me:

'Girl, you are strong, you are fierce and you are meant to be heard.'

THIS IS THE EXCITING PART.

MAKE THE CHANGES YOU WANT TO SEE IN THE WORLD.

BOUNCE BACK

FROM FAILURE

Every campaign in history has failed in some respect, shape or form. Every single one! But that's not to say that such campaigns have failed overall. To the contrary, many have ultimately gone on to succeed.

The End Tampon Tax campaign is no exception.

I AM NO STRANGER TO MISTAKES OR FAILING!

Everyone working on this campaign has faced many setbacks. But we've all learned to bounce back like pros! For example, when I started the campaign I sent letters to my local MP and the chancellor's office asking for their support and advice. I presumed they wouldn't reply. But they did! This is what my local MP said:

Dear Ms Coryton,

Thank you for contacting me about tax on tampons and sanitary towels.

I regret to inform you that it is not within the Government's power to reduce the already discounted 5 per cent rate of VAT charged on women's sanitary products.

This is because VAT law is governed by the EU, with EU legislation determining a very specific set of products which may be zero-rated (have no VAT). The EU does not allow the UK, or any other member state, to extend unilaterally the scope of existing zero rates or to introduce new ones.

Consequently, the current 5 per cent rate of VAT on women's sanitary products is the lowest rate allowed under EU law.

Thank you again for taking the time to contact me.

With best wishes.
Your sincerely,

Mel Stride
Member of Parliament for Central Devon

BOUNCE BACK

Although their responses weren't quite the 'let me change this for you immediately!' letters I had naively imagined, they did give me the information I needed to move forward and take my next campaign steps. They made me realize I needed to do some investigating into the EU as a possible second decision maker and get as many other politicians on side to counteract these less than enthusiastic responses. These letters helped me to hash out my next plan of action. They ended up strengthening my campaign!

Dealing with failure can be difficult, but always keep in mind that you are becoming a trained change-maker. You are awesome. You can solve ANY problem you face.

YOU CAN ALWAYS TURN YOUR SETBACKS INTO SUCCESSES.

Here are my tips for doing just that and bouncing back from campaigning failures:

TIP 1. SPEAK UP

So far we've talked a lot about speaking up by campaigning to instigate changes. That's important! But it's also important to speak up on a personal level when you need help. If you're facing a problem that seems campaign-shattering then do not let it fill you with fear or dread. Do not let it make you feel alone, because you're absolutely not! Talk to your friends, family, community and fellow change-makers about how you're feeling, your problem and how you might overcome it.

Sharing your concerns will not only make you feel better, it will also ensure you tackle your campaign problems as effectively as possible while avoiding any subsequent mishaps. Asking for help or advice is never a bad thing. It may be the key to your campaign's success and strengthen your ability to change the world!

I speak to my ninja twin, family, friends and sister campaigners about my campaigning concerns on an almost daily basis. I am not shy about having questions or doubts. Speaking to them makes me feel better. I can talk through any problems I foresee and at the same time they remind me that I really can instigate my changes no matter what. They give me the fire I need to turn my weaknesses and my bad days into my strengths.

TIP 2. STAY FOCUSED

Campaign failures are a little like hiccups. They are annoying, disruptive and they always happen at a bad time. They can start totally at random and for some people once hiccups begin they can continue for what feels like an eternity!

Campaign failures can also be disruptive. They can consume your thoughts and lead to you making further mistakes as a result. To avoid this, it's important NOT TO PANIC! Stay focused, be positive and remember that like hiccups, campaign mishaps always come to an end sooner or later. One of my best friends Danielle always tell me: 'See every obstacle as a chance for growth.' Always focus on that!

I've experienced campaign hiccups many, many times. The EU referendum was a particularly hiccup-filled period! I've always loved the fact that our tampon tax supporters are members of all political parties, from the Conservatives to Labour. It's a campaign about feminism and periods: two things powerful enough to transcend political biases and interest people of all walks of life. I have worked really hard to make sure all of our supporters feel welcome.

Once the referendum was called it seemed that all of this work had been for nothing. News broke that Nigel Farage had presented himself as the primary political End Tampon Tax campaign backer. This was not helpful as Farage was a very divisive politician, the outspoken leader of UKIP (UK Independence Party). Anyone not a member of UKIP would likely be put off our campaign.

This news not only contradicted the party neutrality that I had worked so hard to sustain, but it also came at a difficult time – during the complex campaigning before the Brexit vote in 2016. Nigel Farage's support made us (End Tampon Tax campaigners) look as though we were utilizing our platform to fuel the Leave vote (which his party supported). This was entirely out of my control. Many of our supporters who were not fans of UKIP were angry at me. The campaign was in jeopardy.

We hadn't asked for any of this to happen. This wasn't in our campaign road-map plan at all! I felt like the world was ending and there was nothing I could do about it.

To overcome this failure I stayed focused. I hashed out a plan of action with the amazing superwomen at change.org and my friends and family. We decided that if we could get one UK party leader to support us, we could get more. We lobbied other political parties extra hard into offering their support for our campaign. This worked! Political neutrality was restored and after team Remain joined our campaign, nobody connected us exclusively with the Leave vote any more. The world (and the campaign) was saved!

Even when circumstances feel out of your hands, remind yourself that things will get better. Trust in your friends, family and sister campaigners. Talk to them. They will help you to conjure up a plan of action!

In the meantime, connect with your supporters. You can explain your situation to them by posting an update (this is a key function of online petition sites, such as change.org. It involves sending an email out to everyone who has signed your petition – it's amazing!). Your supporters will understand. They will be there for you. They are golden.

131

TIP 3. REMEMBER YOU ARE HUMAN

Above all, you need to remember that you are a human being. Succeeding as a strong feminist (or change-maker bossing it in any other sphere) does not mean you have to be superwoman every day of the week. You become no less awesome when something goes wrong. You'll still be a badass change-maker and you're still doing great things. None of that will change.

Having said that, if you do make a mistake and that makes you feel rubbish, that's OK too. It's natural to feel a failure. To get over this feeling make sure you look after yourself and remember that every time you fail you prove the issue you're trying to solve is difficult! You prove that your issue is worth investing lots of time and energy into dealing with. Essentially, you legitimize your work. Even failing can strengthen your campaign!

You also need to remember that the world is an unpredictable place. Failures often won't be your fault, nor will they be foreseeable, but you will be able to overcome them nonetheless. By believing in yourself and your abilities, you can turn failures into your strengths and ultimately, your successes.

TIP 4. IT'S NOT ALL ABOUT WINNING

This is perhaps the BIGGEST and most important tip I have to offer. Do not focus entirely on your one major end goal. Remember that there are other important accomplishments that you will achieve along the way to reaching your ultimate campaign finishing line. Sometimes, you will achieve these amazing things without even realizing!

TOP TIP: When I asked Kajal Odedra, UK change.org director, about the prospect of failing she said: *'One of the most important things in campaigning is solidarity and finding a sense of belonging. It's not all about winning or getting from A to B. It's about enabling people to feel like they belong.'*

Similarly, winning the tampon tax campaign did not rest entirely with ending tampon tax. Along the way we got lots of people talking about periods, from supporters to journalists and politicians! That was a huge win – very few people in public life were talking about periods before that. We celebrated little victories all the time. We revelled in the fact that we were making people feel like they belong in their bodies and that women belong in political conversations.

YOUR TURN

It's worth noting down the smaller important accomplishments that you will make by virtue of campaigning for your change. If your goal takes a while to achieve (and lots do) then referring back to these nuggets of success will help to motivate you to keep going. It will show you that by campaigning for your goal you're already changing the world, irrespective of when you reach your ultimate goal.

REMEMBER, TO BOUNCE BACK FROM FAILURE:

Speak up

Stay focused

Remember you are human!

And don't forget that it's OK to fail

Campaigning is a long road. There are twists and turns – exciting ones and bumpy ones. But if you keep putting one foot in front of the other, you'll make progress.

HAVE FAITH IN YOURSELF AND YOU CAN BOUNCE BACK FROM ANYTHING.

BOUNCE BACK FROM TROLLS

I wish I didn't have to write this section. A few years ago, I wouldn't have had to. Trolls didn't exist. Online ones, I mean – those ogres who live under bridges and terrorize the three Billy Goats Gruff have been around for a long time!

Online trolls are cowardly people who hide behind the anonymity of the internet to attack others on social media. But if you wouldn't say or do it in real life, if something is illegal IRL, why on earth would you think you can do it online and get away with it? But sadly some people troll others, especially those in the public eye.

And if you're going to front a kick-ass campaign to change the world, that means putting yourself out there. You want to attract lots of positive attention and support for your cause – go, you! Unfortunately, some people don't have anything better to do with their time than attack awesome campaigners and so I have to prepare you for it.

First of all, let's get one thing straight:

TROLLING IS WRONG.

As the inspiring Laura Bates, founder of the Everyday Sexism Project, said, 'You could be sitting at home in your living room, outside of working hours, and suddenly someone is able to send you a graphic rape threat right into the palm of your hand.' That is wrong, plain and simple. Social media has opened up the world in so many good ways, but strangers have a much harder time getting into your living room physically than they do over Twitter or other online platforms.

Luckily the law agrees and is catching up. Whenever someone trolls you, they are committing an offence under the Malicious Communications Act. This act is brilliant. It criminalizes anyone who 'sends a letter, electronic communication or article of any description which conveys a message which is indecent or grossly offensive, a threat or information which is false. If the reason for that communication was to cause distress or anxiety to the recipient or to any other person, then the sender is guilty of an offence. The act stands whether those targeted actually receive the message or not.'

Harassment and threatening behaviour is against the law. If you ever feel threatened or harassed online, know that the law is on your side. Moral standards should be the same online as they are offline.

Yet trolling still happens at a staggering rate. The NSPCC has found that a quarter of young people aged 16 or younger have faced race or hate messages online. That's a LOT of people. Know that you can defeat them. You can stop trolls from bringing you down. I know, because I too got trolled.

| | | | | | | | | | |

Here are some of my top troll-slaying tips.
I categorize trolls into Level 1 and Level 2 . . .

LEVEL 1 TROLLS

The annoying accounts that send irritating and hateful messages to awesome women.

Level 1 trolls are a bit milder than Level 2. These trolls mostly send hateful messages to people online simply for being a member of a group (for example, they will send messages to women simply for being women, etc.).

Sometimes Level 1 trolls can prevent us from speaking up. Dealing with trolls can be a horrible and deeply personal experience. If it happens to you or any of your friends, then I am really sorry. You shouldn't have to deal with this kind of abuse. But stay strong. Keep speaking up. Most importantly, never question or doubt yourself or your abilities to solve problems, make things better and change your world. Trolls attack people who are succeeding. If you face trolls, it's because you are powerful. Remember that.

I used to experience Level 1 trolls on a pretty routine basis. Initially this made me pretty upset. I took it personally. I questioned whether speaking up was worth it.

Then I realized something. Trolls demonstrate exactly why we need people like you to speak up. Users that direct hateful messages to specific groups of people simply for speaking up, solving the problems they face and being successful prove that prejudices against them are alive and kicking. Ultimately we can take the energy that trolls invest in taking us down to empower ourselves and to justify the changes that we are trying to make. Trolls embody exactly the hate that our campaigns try to extinguish.

So if someone is trolling you for fighting racism, homophobia or any other prejudice, they too are proving that such prejudices run deep throughout society and harm people. Use their hate as if it were wind to your sails. Let it spur you on to continue your fight and challenge the very normalities that have facilitated the existence of such trolls in the first place.

So how should you deal with trolls if you come across them? Well, this is not an easy question to answer. Firstly, it's important to know that many organizations, including Brooks and the NSPCC, do not recommend responding to trolls. This is because trolls are rarely worth engaging in conversation with. Responding to them can waste time and increase your stress and upset. Essentially, it can give trolls more power. Simply continuing to speak up about your issue in the face of your trolls is perhaps the best way to slay them. Let them fuel your determination to speak up.

If you do ever face trolls, know that you're not alone. JK Rowling is with you. She handles trolling a little differently. To a man who told her to 'stay out of politics' on Twitter, JK tweeted back:

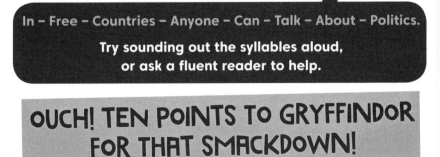

In – Free – Countries – Anyone – Can – Talk – About – Politics.

Try sounding out the syllables aloud, or ask a fluent reader to help.

OUCH! TEN POINTS TO GRYFFINDOR FOR THAT SMACKDOWN!

Superheroes like JK Rowling are defeating trolls (which are scarily similar to he-who-must-not-be-named) so that we don't have to waste our time engaging with them. While she can take away the power of trolls by highlighting their stupidity to the world, we can get on with speaking up about the problems that we face.

If you ever face trolling, remember that you have the power to BLOCK and REPORT the hell out of them.

LEVEL 2 TROLLS

Those who send threats of a serious nature, such as physical violence.

Trolls can send more serious threats to amazing women. If a user sends you a message that worries you, then DO NOT HESITATE to report them to the social media platform upon which they troll and to the police. A zero-tolerance policy to trolling is a good policy to uphold!

It has taken time, and trolling has made the internet a darker place, but there is light in the law. In 2017, the then Home Secretary, Amber Rudd, launched a national online hate crime hub, set up to deal with online abuse and trolling. Amber Rudd said this hub has since ensured 'those who commit these cowardly crimes are met with the full force of the law.'

Even the prime minister, Theresa May, has argued that trolling needs to end. In 2018, she said that users of media platforms such as Twitter and Facebook could become open to abuse and that this threat was not only a threat to individuals, but to democracy as a whole.

She then launched a new independent review into dealing with trolls among other online offenders, which aimed to ensure laws protect people online as much as they do offline. I'm sure it's no coincidence that it took a female prime minister and home secretary to legally oppose trolls . . .

The point is that the law's response to trolling is constantly being improved. Reporting trolls is not about getting revenge or seeking anything for yourself. It's about ensuring that you are safe, and that these people do not go on to threaten anybody else and that others understand their behaviour is seriously not OK, ever. It's about ensuring people are protected so that they can speak up and make the world better.

Despite these grand announcements and the law being well and truly on our side, it's actually really difficult to find any advice on exactly what online behaviour the law deems not acceptable and how we are meant to deal with it. Essentially, it's tricky to know exactly when and HOW we can take action. Here's what I've learned from my – unfortunately – extensive experience:

ACTION ON TROLLS

To clear up any confusion here's what we can report:

1. Online comments that intend to be cruel, racist, homophobic, sexist or which incite hatred or violence upon a person or entity.

2. Online comments that intend to damage someone's reputation or business, unless they are factually correct.

3. *The creation of a hashtag for the purpose of sparking an online harassment campaign, or the encouragement of re-tweeting a 'grossly offensive message'.*

4. *Posting someone's home address or bank details online.*

5. *Discussing someone's sexual activity online with the intention to humiliate them.*

6. *The creation and posting of 'disturbing or sinister' Photoshopped images of someone online.*

If you have experienced any of the above, here's what you can do about it:

1. *Collect evidence. Save screenshots of all your troll's comments/messages/images. This is important. It ensures you have all the evidence you might need to prove your troll has acted inappropriately (i.e. done anything listed above). You may later need these screenshots if requested by your social media platform or the police if you want to report them. Whether you decide to report them or not, it's still a good idea to collate these screenshots, just in case you need them at any point in the future.*

2. *Block your troll on social media. This will not only stop your troll from contacting you, it will also remind you that you have power online and that you can determine who gets to contact you. Usually Twitter, Instagram or Facebook have a blocking function accessible on the page of the person or user you wish to block.*

3. *Report your troll to the social media platform they have used to contact or harass you. This will let the platform know that there is a problem. Usually, you can report someone on Twitter, Instagram or Facebook by accessing the report function on the page of the person or user you need to report. The social media site should then respond to your report by deleting their account and ensuring they cannot troll anybody else. Keep a record of when you did this, in case you need it later.*

4. *Call the police. Never hesitate to call the police if a troll has attacked you online. You can reach them 24 hours a day on their non-emergency number, 101. This will connect you to a police officer who can record your experience of online abuse and ensure the correct legal procedures are taken against your troll.*

BOUNCE BACK

I hope this chapter has given you the confidence to speak up without fear of trolling. You now have the weapons you need to slay any trolls that come your way! I've added a list of organizations that exist to help and support young people who are being harassed or threatened online at the back of this book. Use these contacts if you ever need help. They are amazing and they are ALWAYS there for you, no matter what.

SPEAK UP EVERY DAY

Let's not forget that the internet is our superpower. Yes, there are downsides to anonymity online and, yes, I'm afraid you should be prepared for some unpleasantness if you're going to launch an awesome campaign online. BUT it's not all bad! The internet has given power and a platform to people who previously had none.

Nowhere has this been more evident than in the astounding progress made by the Me Too movement. In 2017, countless brave women spoke up about sexual assault. Something very difficult to talk about, something that until now was often swept under the carpet.

It all started when sexual assault allegations piled up sky-high against Hollywood producer Harvey Weinstein. This shook the world. Then one of his biggest critics, actor Alyssa Milano, spoke up. She changed the world. She encouraged women to share their experiences of sexual harassment, while using the Me Too hashtag, to showcase its widespread gravity.

And it did. Within days, MILLIONS of people utilized our superpower, the internet. They galvanized the power of Twitter, Facebook and Instagram by tweeting and posting '#MeToo' across social media to showcase the scale of sexual assaults taking place around the WORLD. The effects of these amazing women and men who spoke up against sexual assault has been incredibly empowering.

TOP TIP: The phrase 'Me Too' was coined by American activist Tarana Burke as a campaign over ten years before Alyssa Milano took up the rallying cry. This shows the power of key influencers in your campaign – one tweet or show of support from someone with vast reach can make your campaign go viral. It also proves that the campaigning superwomen of today stand tall on the shoulders of those who spoke up before them. Use the strength of such women to propel your own messages and ability to make changes today.

The Me Too movement has had a massive impact all over the world. The idea that powerful people can do whatever they want simply because they are powerful has been shattered by the sheer scale of sexual assaults revealed by the monumental Me Too movement.

IT HAS GIVEN POWER TO SURVIVORS.

#METOO

#METOO

There's still a long way to go to combat sexual assault, but this campaign has done a LOT to tackle the issue. What the Me Too movement tells us is that, first, women everywhere can take power from their experiences and that with the support of other women, we are unstoppable. Secondly, it shows us that our personal experiences and everyday actions, such as posting something online or talking to friends about issues, are political. The Me Too movement proves that everyday campaigning acts are just as effective as any other.

EVERYDAY ACTIONS MAKE A DIFFERENCE. THEY EMPOWER US. THEY CHANGE THE WORLD.

SPEAK UP EVERY DAY

THE PERSONAL IS POLITICAL

Until now we've been focusing on speaking up in the context of a big campaign or taking public action. But as we've seen throughout this book so far, all these big issues and -isms not only impact the world at large – they impact our everyday lives.

Speaking up on an everyday basis by talking to your friends, family and those around you about the issues that you think are important might seem like a strange or ineffective way to make a difference, compared to a big campaign. But the Me Too movement proves that it shouldn't. It's a subtle but poignant and extremely punchy way to campaign.

WHY? BECAUSE OUR PERSONAL EXPERIENCES ARE POLITICAL.

They not only inspire us and (hopefully) others to launch great big campaigns, but our everyday actions also work to combat prejudices. They challenge assumptions and change narratives. You're probably already doing this: you get your little cousin a garage for her birthday, but your uncle laughs and says she'd prefer a doll's house.

You say, WHY? Why can't girls play with cars? Or you've just turned vegan and your grandma dismisses it as nonsense. Instead of rolling your eyes, you take the time to explain your reasons.

LITTLE CHALLENGES LIKE THIS CAN MAKE THE BIGGEST IMPRESSIONS.

REMEMBER: Ripples become waves. It's not always the loudest campaigns that make the biggest difference.

I want you to feel empowered to take on -isms in everyday interactions. Sometimes this can feel even more daunting than taking a big campaign into the wider world. Speaking up on an everyday basis involves challenging people you know in your day-to-day life, face to face. So buckle up and get ready for my road trip to Self-Confidence Town and

SPEAKING UP EVERY DAY!

RELATIONSHIPS

To make sure you're confident enough to take on the world and secure some serious changes, first you need to feel comfortable and in control of all aspects of your life. This includes those tricky parts, such as relationships.

DUN DUN DUNNN

Let's begin by talking about the most important relationships you'll have in your life: your friends and family.
My best friend Gussie once told me:

'While romances come and go, your true soulmates are often found in your best friends.'

FRIENDS ARE FOREVER.

They will always be there for you, no matter how your campaign is doing. Their continuous support alone will give you the fire you need to defiantly campaign through all kinds of terrain!

HAVE A THINK ABOUT YOUR FRIENDSHIP ROYALTY.

It's these awesome soulmates that change your life and give you the power you need to kick ass. Make sure to treasure the people who support and encourage you to be you and campaign for any changes YOU want to see. Make sure you support and encourage them right back.

Just like we saw in the Me Too movement,

WHEN GIRLS SUPPORT GIRLS WE ALL BECOME UNSTOPPABLE.

As for family, sure, they can be annoying sometimes (maybe a lot of times – and, believe me, I know – battles with my ninja twin sister have often been brutal!), but remember, even if you go through challenging times, your family wants the best for you. And when they see you being a campaigning genius, they'll be first at your demo

WAVING PLACARDS FOR YOU!

NOW LET'S TALK ABOUT ROMANCE.

Some people aren't bothered about having any kind of sexual relationships at all. That's entirely OK. You're not missing out on anything if you don't want a traditional 'partner'. Your friends and family are your soulmates and unconditional campaign supporters. Nothing is going to change that.

Others like having lots of partners. Whether you aren't interested in romance, have lots of partners, or something in between, you're a rock star. You are free to live your life however you want to, with as many or as few partners as you want, period.

CHAPTER 4

Whatever you're interested in, navigating the world of dating in a way that suits YOU and complements your campaigning can be really tricky. So here are my top tips for totally conquering dating:

TOP DATING TIP FOR CAMPAIGNERS
1) FAIRY TALES AREN'T REAL

Fairy tales are eternal classics. Disney made a bunch of them super popular. *Hercules*, *Beauty and the Beast* and *Snow White* are just a few of our favourites.

THESE STORIES INTRODUCE US TO DEEP CONCEPTS, LIKE 'LOVE' AND 'BETRAYAL'.

But if we really think about it, most fairy tales portray a pretty bizarre and idealized form of these concepts that can lead us to have unrealistic and unhealthy expectations of love. Expectations that do NOT support dreams of female campaigning superstardom AT ALL. *BOOS*

Think about it. Think about your favourite fairy-tale film. Does it incorporate the idea that men ultimately save women, who are otherwise perpetually damned, incomplete by themselves and certainly incapable of instigating serious changes? Even Hercules (my fave) does!!

THIS PLOT HAS MANY PROBLEMS. LEAST OF ALL, IT'S NOT REAL!

First, this model of love emphasizes a deeply gendered power imbalance. Male fairy-tale protagonists tend to be powerful, courageous and full of agency. They can pretty much do whatever they like and remain a hero/complete competent character regardless. This gives us the message that men in real, everyday life are also inherently powerful, complete and competent by virtue of being men. They're usually rich, tall and very athletic too – how's that for boys to live up to? On the other hand, leading female fairy-tale characters are usually lacking in agency – that means being in control of making choices for themselves.

THEY OFTEN RELY ON THE POWER INNATELY HELD BY A LEADING MALE CHARACTER

(e.g. the Prince in *Sleeping Beauty*) to free them from the grasp of powerlessness and incompetence (e.g. Aurora being asleep), after which they are eternally indebted to their male saviours (e.g. oo thanks for kissing me and waking me up, which I didn't ask for!!).

Since we see this plot over and over and OVER, we take in the message that women in general are lacking in power.

THEY CAN'T CHOOSE
THEIR OWN DESTINY.

They can't influence major political policies. They can't speak up on an everyday basis. Not only that, but they are also perpetually reliant on the power of men to transform them into fully functioning characters. Basically it suggests that women are defined by their male counterpart, while men define themselves.   This diminishes female power and our ability to

The point is, do not get sucked in by fairy-tale fakeness.

YOU CAN DO AND BE WHATEVER AND WHOEVER YOU WANT.

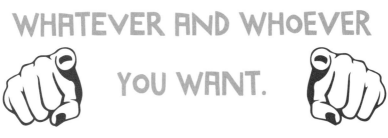

Just like any fairy-tale hero, you have the power to run any campaign you want, all by yourself. Oh, and let's make one other pretty crucial thing clear: you don't need fairy-tale guys, or any romantic partner at all, to secure campaigning success – or any kind of success for that matter! Your partner can be an amazing supporter just like anyone else, but they don't give you the power you need to campaign like a true hero. That power is already yours, no matter what.

TOP DATING TIP FOR CAMPAIGNERS
2) YOUR HAPPINESS IS YOUR BUSINESS, NOBODY ELSE'S

First, here's when and why you should ask someone out (yes, girls should totally ask out whoever they want, whenever they want):

1. Because you want to.
2. Literally no other reason.

Reasons not to ask someone out:

1. Because they have more Marmite than you do and you want to steal their supplies (although this is totally understandable, it's not really OK).
2. You've finally found someone who enjoys *South Park* just as much as you do and confuse this with love at first episode (I may or may not be speaking from experience . . .).
3. Because you hope being in a relationship with someone will make you happy.

This last point is a really serious one.

It's important to remember that your happiness is all your own. Depending on someone else to make you happy is problematic. Similarly, nobody else should hinge their happiness on you. If they did, they would put a LOT of pressure on you. It would be really unfair. When you hinge your happiness on yourself YOU are in control. You have power.

TOP DATING TIP FOR CAMPAIGNERS
3) THERE IS NO 'RIGHT' DATE

This tip might sound obvious, but it's important:

EVERYBODY DATES DIFFERENTLY.

Basically, be yourself. You are in control. If you enjoy movies, go on dates to the movies. If you don't, then don't! Date whoever you like, wherever you like, however you like. Do what makes you happy. Tailor your dating experience to your own preferences, and nobody else's. There is no 'dating fits all' guide. As my mama always says, 'a date is whatever you want it to be!'

TOP DATING TIP FOR CAMPAIGNERS
4) BEING SINGLE IS AWESOME!

This last point is something I live by. It's inspired by activist, author and idol to many, Chimamanda Ngozi Adichie, who made this perfect observation in her 2012 Ted Talk 'We Should All Be Feminists': (To watch the full talk, visit TED.com)

'A woman at a certain age who is unmarried, our society teaches her to see it as a deep personal failure. And a man at a certain age who is unmarried, we just think he hasn't come around to making his pick.'

Society tends to reflect Disney nonsense probably more than we realize. It is often assumed that single women are helpless damsels. That they're failing their presumed sole purpose in life, to be a wife and/or a mother, and that therefore they're failing as a person.

NEWSFLASH

Women can be totally awesome wives and mothers, but they can also be amazing campaigners and change the world without a ring or a child. Your ability to succeed as a person and an influential campaigner has nothing whatsoever to do with your relationship status. Remember that your happiness is yours. Your confidence is yours. Neither depend on any other person.

The media often perpetuates this idea. Reporters are STILL asking Hollywood's biggest female stars about baby names (irrespective of whether such celebs actually plan to have babies or not . . .), which designers they're 'totally into right now' and what their 'relationship secrets' are. *yawns* And if they aren't interested in having babies or relationships because, let's face it, they're pretty busy conquering the entire film industry, aren't they sad about it? These often multi award-winning queens of Hollywood.

My sister Julia always reminds me that we should always be who and what WE want to be.

Neither of these things depend on your relationship status. They simply depend on you being awesome, kick-ass, brilliant campaigning you! If you're in a relationship, you don't equate to one half of a whole. You've always constituted a whole wonderful, valuable and POWERFUL being.

ALL BY YOURSELF.

CONSENT

We've talked about sexual assaults and empowerment in the context of the Me Too movement, but what does speaking up about these issues look like on an everyday basis? How does this political movement show itself in your personal life? Well, there's one word for this: consent. By speaking up about consent, you're empowering those around you. In my work in schools I get a lot of questions about consent. So, to clear up any confusion and to make sure you're confident about consent, here are my Mastermind-style answers to those top questions:

WHAT IS CONSENT?

To give consent is to give permission. When we talk about consent in the context of sexual relationships we are talking about giving permission for something sexual – from holding hands and kissing all the way to having sex with someone.

You have the power to control the things that you want to do. If someone wants to kiss you, but you don't want this, it's completely OK for you to speak up and tell that person not to kiss you. This means anyone: from your best friend to the cute person in your English class! No matter what, you always have the right to slow down or stop any situation entirely. Doing so is nothing to be embarrassed or ashamed of. It's about using your power and taking control. It's about speaking up!

Consent isn't just about giving permission for how a situation might begin. Ongoing consent is important. Giving permission for someone to kiss you (which is also completely OK!) gives permission for that person to kiss you. That is it. It does not imply permission for that person to have sex with you, or anything else. Only consenting to sex implies consent to sex, and even then you have every right to withdraw this consent at any moment.

WHO IS AT FAULT FOR SEXUAL ASSAULTS?

There is only one person who is ever at fault for a sexual assault: the assaulter. The survivor of assault is never, ever to blame.

DO YOU NEED A REASON TO SAY 'NO'?

Absolutely not! Simply not wanting to do something is reason enough not to do it. You NEVER have to explain yourself. If you kiss someone you fancy in your class today, but don't feel like kissing them tomorrow, that's totally fine. Do whatever you feel is right for YOU at the time and nobody else.

HOW DO YOU KNOW WHAT YOU WANT TO DO?

There is a great rule I've discovered for this. If you're asking yourself whether you really want to do something or not, you're probably unsure and therefore don't want to do whatever it is.

If you think you are ready to do whatever it is, always ask yourself three important questions just to make sure:

1 Are you enthusiastic about whatever it is you are thinking of doing?

2 Do you feel comfortable?

3 Are you safe in your situation?

CHAPTER 4

If the answer to all three of these questions is a big fat 'YES' then totally go for it if your partner feels the same. If you're not completely sure about any one of these aspects, wait until you are. If you have any doubt whatsoever, wait until you don't! It's as simple as that.

This is a rule you can keep for life. Consent is important irrespective of your age or relationship status. It's crucial to everyone, whether you're single, in a long-term relationship or anything in-between. You always have ultimate control and POWER over your body. Nothing will take this away from you: not a proposal, not marriage, not even a gift. Nothing!

WHO SHOULD BE ASKED FOR THEIR CONSENT?

Everyone! Girls, boys, women, men, people of all genders, ages and sexualities. Nobody is excluded from their right to consent and nothing can exclude you from this right either.

WHAT DO YOU DO IF YOU HAVE FACED SEXUAL ASSAULT?

If you've faced a sexual assault, lots of organizations are here for you. Reporting your incident to the police is really important if you feel comfortable about doing so. Please see the back of the book for more details. Some survivors don't feel able to report an incident of sexual assault to the police right away, or even at all.

But there are plenty of understanding people out there for you. There are lots of organizations dedicated to supporting you regardless. Some of these amazing charities are listed on p222.

DO TALK TO SOMEONE.

DON'T EVER FEEL ALONE.

SIDENOTE ON SEXTING

This is a very modern romantic conundrum. It certainly wasn't around as an issue for your parents, or even for some of your older cousins! If your parents have tried to talk to you about it, good for them, but more likely they haven't because they're embarrassed and don't understand it. You're probably relieved, because that would be SUCH an embarrassing conversation, right?

WELL, DON'T WORRY BECAUSE THIS IS A SAFE SPACE. LET'S TALK ALL THINGS SEXTING.

In many ways sexting is a lot like sex in real life. YOU are in control. You can decide how far you want to take it.

But sometimes sexting can get out of hand. If you are thinking about sharing nude images with anyone online, there are some serious things you need to be aware of. First, it is illegal to share, create, possess or distribute nude images of anyone under the age of 18. This means you'll be committing a crime, but it also means that if the person you decide to share images with keeps them or sends them to anyone else, they too will be committing an offence. If you feel that someone is pressuring you into sending them anything you're uncomfortable with, then you can block them, report them and even call the police. Pressuring anyone into sending nude or provocative images is pressuring them into committing an offence. That's never OK. The law is always on your side. Take POWER in that.

Keep in mind that you're in control of your body. It's never OK for anyone to pressure you into doing anything you're not comfortable with. If you decide to send a video, image or message online, remember that once you hit 'send' your content is out of your control. Even if you trust the person you are sending it to, things can change. If it is shared online it may feel awful, but you still have POWER. You can speak up. You can tell someone who can help.

Here are just a few amazing sites set up to support you. DO check them out for any more advice:

https://cyberbullying.org/sexting-advice-teens
https://www.nspcc.org.uk/preventing-abuse/
keeping-children-safe/sexting/

SELF-LOVE

Now you've got lots of information about consent and are armed with the tips to conquer the world of dating while also ensuring your campaigning thrives, it's time to discuss the MOST IMPORTANT step to achieving unwavering confidence and ensuring you're ready to make changes:

SELF-LOOOOOOVE!

Put yourself first, always respect and embrace yourself and never feel like you have to be somebody else to succeed.

YOU ARE YOU. YOU ARE TALENTED. YOU ARE AWESOME. YOU CAN MAKE SERIOUS CHANGES.

A campaign race is long and hard. You need to take care of yourself to be the best campaigner you can be.

THIS IS A CALL TO ACTION.

A call to be kind to yourself, to be thoughtful and mindful of what you need. Let's make sure girls like you are confident enough to put themselves first while stepping up, speaking up and campaigning.

LET'S REFOCUS PERSPECTIVES

ON SELF-LOVE

ONCE AND FOR ALL.

Maybe you already know your worth and you are werk-ing it. (You go, girl!) But if you are anything like me as a teenager, you might have a few tiny (how about huge) self-confidence issues. To help you get to a place where you are comfortable with yourself and feel able to lead your own campaign I want to talk about the astonishing painter and political activist Frida Kahlo. In many ways she pioneered the concept of female self-love.

Frida was an extraordinary artist. She also had polio as a child and then literally to add insult to injury was in a horrific traffic accident. She suffered from many health issues throughout her life and was often confined to her bed. But this didn't stop Frida from becoming one of the most important artists of her time – and our time.

SHE LET HER LIFE EXPERIENCES FUEL HER PASSIONS AND HER FIRE.

She was inspired by herself and refused self-pity. She was fascinated by her body AND her inner life and produced many powerful self-portraits.

Frida proclaimed herself her own muse, the subject she knew best. To me, she embraced all things self-loveee!

SHE. WAS.

AMAZING.

For someone who let her tragedies inspire her achievements (which were plentiful!) Frida would want you to feel crazy confidence in yourself and your abilities. She would not want you to be held back by those societal norms that trickle down from great big '-isms' to affect your daily life. The sexism that powers magazine headlines to 'get a bikini body' can make us think that's more important than eating healthily and taking care of ourselves. It's not!

REMEMBER: THE PERSONAL

IS THE POLITICAL.

Here are some Frida Kahlo-inspired observations on societal norms that hold women back today:

OBSERVATION TO OBLITERATE
1) YOUR 'BEST' BODY

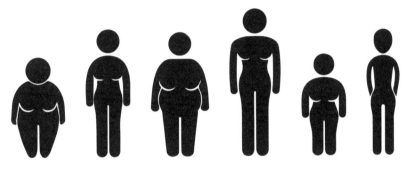

For years magazines and social media sites have been promoting the idea that you can get your 'best' body by eating raw kale ten times an hour, gyming while you sleep and climbing Mount Everest on a Tuesday afternoon.

While this might be fun for some people, for most of us, it isn't fun, it's not realistic and it's SUPER distracting from all of the other actually legitimate goals we have – like leading our own world-shattering campaigns and all!

First, let's dissect exactly what a 'best' body is. It seems to be the product of an idea.

THIS IDEA IS THAT WOMEN'S BODIES ARE SOMEHOW PUBLIC PROPERTY.

Anything in the public domain is open to public commenting, alteration and criticism. Our 'best' body is something that others are allowed to comment on, because our bodies take up public space – how dare we?! And if our bodies don't please totally random passers-by or match up to some idea someone saw in a magazine, then, well, of course the public at large should tell us off!

TOP TIP: Just think, the ridiculous number of hours that you are meant to dedicate to blending kale with special oats while forever gyming could be spent doing other possibly more awesome things like slaying trolls online or, you know, changing the world through campaigning . . .

The truth is, your 'best' body is the very opposite of an idealized public concept. In fact, your 'best' body is the body you already have.

IT'S BRILLIANT, FABULOUS, AWESOME AND KICK-ASS. IT'S YOU!

You belong to one person and one person only: yourself. Nobody has the right to comment on your body. Don't let anybody tell you otherwise.

Emma Watson reiterates this point time and time again. She's often telling journalists who comment on her body that it doesn't matter what she looks like. What matters is what she's doing, changing and speaking up about.

BOOM!

Be confident about the body you have. No matter your weight, your stretch marks (fact: they are totally normal and lots of people have them) or your age, your body is a trooper. It keeps you alive and able to experience the world in the way you so brilliantly do. It allows you to campaign! It gives you POWER. Celebrate it. Be body positive. Accept yourself for who you are now.

YOU'RE FREAKING AWESOME AS YOU ARE. OWN THAT.

OBSERVATION TO OBLITERATE
2) BEAUTY STANDARDS

This brings me on to a short history of beauty. Bear with me, I swear it's good!

BELIEVE IT OR NOT, 'BEAUTY' IS ENTIRELY MADE-UP.

Not even Zeus, king of the gods in ancient Greece, decided at the beginning of time what constituted a beautiful face or body and what did not. We made that decision. As a result that weird thing we call 'beauty standards' is always changing in a pretty striking way.

So if someone ever tells you to shut up and stop campaigning because you don't fit the beauty 'norm' (seriously, this weird and illogical argument has been made to me and sadly many others) then you don't have to go straight to your ninja sister for backup. Instead let them know that THEIR beauty standards have simply NOTHING to do with you or your ability to make campaigning waves.

And by the way,

BEAUTY 'NORMS' ARE ALWAYS DRAMATICALLY CHANGING.

So there's simply no point in paying any attention to them. At all. If anyone tries to use them against you, here's a brief history lesson you can recite to prove that beauty standards are ever-changing and therefore TOTALLY irrelevant.

Throughout the Renaissance and Baroque eras (1600–1700s) female beauty was all about size. Women were celebrated for their large and voluptuous figures. The more curves, rolls and

cellulite, the merrier. During the Victorian era (1800s) having a tiny waist and big bum was all the rage. Corsets (there's a whole heap of feminist analysis for this really damaging contraption!), petticoats, hoops and bustles were all used on an everyday basis. Women would wear these unhealthy and sometimes life-threatening pieces to adhere to the beauty standards that society chose to impose on to them at the time. If that doesn't sound wrong, I don't know what does.

In the 1920s beauty standards changed again.

FEMINISM WAS BEGINNING TO TAKE OVER.

This impacted on the fashion industry. Women started to design and make their own garments. Women spoke up. Practical and loose-fitting clothes were in.

There are many, many major problems with the fact that beauty and body standards are perpetually changing. From my potted history, can't you see they've been anything BUT 'standard', changing every few years?! But perhaps the most striking problem is that although 'popular' body shapes have changed over time, some things have remained standard. Throughout history the same women have been repeatedly excluded: those over a certain age, of different races, religions, body abilities and sexualities always seem to be deemed outside the 'ideal'. Basically beauty standards are just ANOTHER way women have been silenced and kept from speaking up. This needs to stop.

WE NEED TO SPEAK UP ABOUT IT!

TOP TIP: Next time you overhear someone judging a woman for her body, tell them to stop reinforcing the beauty standards that exclude most races, ages and bodies. Channel your inner athlete Serena Williams by celebrating your body, just like I think she does so powerfully and unapologetically.

OBSERVATION TO OBLITERATE
3) BODY 'TYPES' (THEY AREN'T REAL!)

Apples, pears and bananas are all different kinds of the same thing: fruit. They belong in the fruit bowl, not the wardrobe. Yet for generations the media has been telling us that we have body 'types' that resemble these fruits, and depending on which one best describes our bodies, we should dress accordingly. Literally none of this makes any sense. Since when do women's bodies relate at all to fruit and why are we dressing these fruit, anyway? It's super weird. It needs to stop.

SPEAK UP EVERY DAY

The point is that you can dress however the hell you like.

FEEL CONFIDENT WEARING ANYTHING YOU LIKE.

Don't be categorized or told that you shouldn't show certain parts of your body to the world for some bizarre and illogical fruit-related reason. You show whatever part of your body you want to show, whenever and however you want to show it. If someone ever tells you otherwise, you can kindly remind them that actually your body doesn't belong to them (SHOCK!). Your body is all yours and nobody else's. You have the right to love your body and dress however you like. End of story. Oh, and don't forget to ask them if they can stop judging women just because they're women, please?

SMILES SARCASTICALLY

OBSERVATION TO OBLITERATE
4) RULES OF HOW TO PUT YOUR MAKE-UP ON

Put make-up on whenever and however you want to. Wow, that was a short tutorial!

FINAL OBSERVATION:
YOUR VALUE

There's a message that beauty standards convey. This message is the most dangerous of them all: beauty standards are seen to define a woman's value in the world. If a woman is deemed to be beautiful (whatever that may mean at the time) then she is presumed to be worth more than those who are not deemed to be beautiful and as a result, her very life is assumed to be more precious.

THIS MAKES NO SENSE WHATSOEVER.

Not only do fluctuating beauty standards make this an impossible test to pass consistently, but the very idea that women should pass some sort of beauty test to establish any life value is ridiculous. It reduces women. It stops them from speaking out. It keeps women in an inescapable state of oppression that ensures they have no control over the value or direction of their life.

IT'S ABSOLUTE RUBBISH.

It's something we need to fight. So, finally, let's end on perhaps the most important point of this chapter on self-confidence, body positivity and self-love:

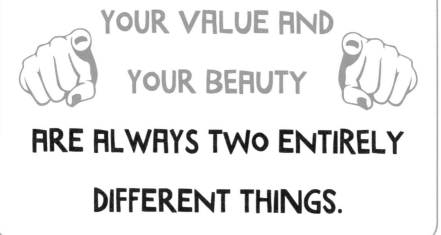

YOUR VALUE AND YOUR BEAUTY ARE ALWAYS TWO ENTIRELY DIFFERENT THINGS.

Your ability to campaign, make changes and be confident is totally unrelated to fruit or, perhaps more importantly, to beauty standards.

None other than Beyoncé is queen of self-love. Whenever I feel self-conscious or concerned about the way that I look, I remember that Beyoncé focuses her energy on something bigger than beauty: being ICONIC.

To channel your inner Bey, you can do the same. To fight back against beauty standards, forget about being 'hot' (whatever that means in the moment). Focus on you. Be iconic, change the world by speaking (or singing!) up and empowering yourself and other women.

YOU GO, GIRL!

YOUR NEXT STEPS AND KICKING ASS

Imagine a future world where anything is possible. Half of the world's political leaders could be women creating new policies and laws that benefit other women. Imagine how awesome that world would be! Such a world doesn't have to feel so far away – don't take anything for granted. Anything can happen because this is YOUR future and it's one hell of a bright place. Just like my mama always tells me:

'YOUR FUTURE IS IN YOUR HANDS.'

Think of the past few years. Just think of how much campaigning has changed! Thanks to women who had the confidence to speak up, France has introduced harsher punishments for catcalling. Saudi Arabia has passed a law allowing women to drive for the first time in the country's history. India has axed tampon tax and women's marches have exploded across the world, showcasing the power of women and their commitment to speaking up. Such power was so clearly demonstrated by the millions of women who bravely spoke up across the world about sexual abuse as part of many campaigns, including the Me Too movement. They changed the way we view sexual harassment and redefined female power.

All of this and SO much more has happened in just a few years. Imagine what you can do with the years to come.

IMAGINE WHAT
YOU CAN CHANGE.

SO WHAT'S NEXT FOR YOU?

We've talked about how to become a kick-ass campaigner, how to bounce back from failure and how to speak up in everyday life. We're ready to take over the world! But which next steps are best for you? How do you decide which choices to make about the many paths you could go down in the next few years? What path will you take on your road to speaking up?

Activism might become the central work of your life. Or it might be more of a side hustle on your road to greatness. Both work, both are awesome, both can make amazing change. Right now, you have several choices. Do you:

1. Go to university?
2. Take a vocational course, like a BTEC or one of the new T levels?
3. Take up an apprenticeship, a degree apprenticeship or a higher apprenticeship?
4. Launch yourself straight into the world of work?

Throughout your life you will come across lots of opportunities. Some will help you to solve the different problems that people face, including those that affect you. Always carefully consider these opportunities and never let them overwhelm you. You never know where they might take you. Here are just a few of such opportunities that you might want to explore, if you haven't already done so:

EDUCATION

Access to education is so important. It can really strengthen your campaigning work. BUT it's far from guaranteed in so many parts of the world. While going to school may be a normal part of life for many of us, others across the world are denied an education. Often this is simply because they are girls. Amazing campaigner and Nobel Peace Prize winner Malala Yousafzai changed the world when she spoke up about this. Growing up in Pakistan, she was denied an education because she is a girl. But she made noise. She campaigned. She took action. She proved how amazing girls can be and what a difference a single voice can make.

We should never forget how lucky we are that it's assumed and encouraged that we all go to school until at least the age of 16 if not 18. More than that, over half of us go on to further study or college, and a third of all school leavers in the UK do go on to university. This is one of the highest percentages in the entire world!

Simply having the choice to go to university at any point in our lives is like a diamond we should always treasure, especially because women haven't always had access to higher education. In fact, many individuals, organizations and institutions prevented women from attending university for centuries. But women spoke up. They campaigned and campaigned until universities admitted women on to their degree programmes. In doing so they changed the future. They made the future female.

THEY CHANGED THE WORLD!

Going to university can be amazing. It can feed your curiosity, boost your confidence and arm you with the skills you need to take on the world. There are LOTS of opportunities to test out your campaigning toolkit there too. There are debating societies where you can hone your powers of persuasion. There are student unions where you can run a campaign to get elected into office. Maybe you want to become a career politician – university is a great training ground for that.

You can also side hustle a campaign (or two!) on any number of issues. For example, when I studied at Oxford there were two huge and opposing movements around the existence of Cecil Rhodes' statue. Cecil Rhodes was a key figure during the time of the British Empire. On one side, some students and staff thought the statue an important part of the university's history – a representation of freedom of thought and central to some £100m in gifts, including the Rhodes Scholarship. On the other side, 'Rhodes Must Fall' student campaigners deemed it inappropriate to celebrate the statue of an imperialist that they argued represents Britain's 'Imperial blind spot' and organized demos in support of taking it down. It was an incredible time to see two such vibrant sides of debate so prominent in student life.

Ultimately the 'Rhodes Must Fall' campaign has not yet succeeded. Oxford's Oriel College have announced their desire to keep the statue but the debate continues as campaigners are still fighting to secure this change and the long-term future of Rhodes' statue remains unknown . . .

If you're excited about exploring subjects and theories you may have never even imagined before, viewing the world in new and challenging ways, and maybe even feel this will strengthen your campaigning FIRE, then nothing should hold you back from gaining a university education. Nothing!

ALWAYS REACH FOR THE TOP

and don't let anybody stop you from studying what excites and intrigues you. Nothing should get in the way of you and your education.

It's worth questioning whether you would like to study something related to your campaign, so that your studies strengthen your lobbying work, or something entirely different so that you have distance between the two. I chose to integrate the two, by taking an MA in Women's Studies and found it really helpful to devote all of my time to tackling the same general -ism, but you might find it more helpful to spread your interests. You might also want to consider taking a degree that involves work experience in your campaigning field and/or taking a sandwich year working as part of your degree. You can always integrate work and study. Don't ever feel like you have to choose just one.

Finally keep in mind studying at university can be difficult, even for a brilliant campaigner. Wherever and whichever subject you choose to study, everybody faces challenges. For some people, these can be financial. Taking on student debt is a daunting prospect but it is more like a graduate tax. You'll only pay it back if you're earning over a certain amount, and even then your repayments will be a fraction of your earnings. Don't be put off by anything if you feel this is the path for you.

There are other problems students might face. For me, it was missing my twin. I had shared everything with Julia and suddenly, I was alone. But I spoke up. I talked to my family, friends and flatmates about how I was feeling and I soon embraced my own company. If you ever face problems, you can overcome them too by speaking up and using your voice!

TRAINING AND APPRENTICESHIPS

There's more to education than university, which isn't for everyone. Not going to university doesn't mean that you're letting down the women who fought for your right to a higher education. Not at all! Those women fought for you to CHOOSE whether you will personally benefit from university or not.

YOU NEED TO CHOOSE WHAT IS RIGHT FOR YOU.

That's one of the most powerful choices you can make.

There are many other opportunities out there, like starting an apprenticeship or training course. These are amazing if you want to learn new skills and be trained specifically for a chosen industry. You can find apprenticeship opportunities in lots of different sectors. And I mean, LOTS. From creative and media opportunities, to apprenticeships in business, administrative and accounting, environmental sciences, engineering and IT, healthcare, social care, animal care and education, retail, tourism, hospitality, transport, logistics, sport and leisure. Whatever your interest, there's an apprenticeship for you.

Apprenticeships can be a great way to learn and earn at the same time. Britain has a skills shortage and the government has levied a new tax called the Apprenticeship Levy on larger firms to fund training schemes. There is money available for apprenticeships that you can benefit from. Yes, you!

And remember, you don't have to become a politician to make politics front and centre in your adult life. Many industries have unions that recruit representatives from their members and workers. It can be an amazing way to get involved in campaigning at grassroots level, support your coworkers and make real change in your local community.

WORK (#WERK)

Whether you start right now, or after a few more years in education, your whole career is ahead of you.

YOU CAN BE ANYTHING

YOU WANT TO BE!

Remember our lessons in self-confidence, because even now, even after all the progress that we have made, the working world can seem like an alien place for women. To conquer all working environments there are a few things you need to keep in mind:

THE PAY GAP

According to the Office for National Statistics, across the UK employed women in 2018 typically earned 17.9 per cent less than men. This difference in earnings has been dubbed a gender pay gap.

WHY DOES THE PAY GAP MATTER?

Well, it matters because it suggests that somehow women are worth or valued less than men in the workplace.

The situation is improving: the pay gap is slowly reducing. But there's still a long way to go. In fact, if the pay gap continues to close at the same rate it has been since 1960, then we will have to wait until 2059 to finally be paid the same as men. And that's if we ignore the fact that since 2001, progress in equalizing wages has been particularly slow. If we take that into account and presume progress will continue at the rate it has been since 2001, then women won't achieve equal pay until 2119. That's one hell of a long way away!

So what can you do about the pay gap? First, you can be aware of it. Questioning your wage after you secure a job and asking if your male colleagues are paid the same as you is not a crime. Asking your HR department if you are paid the same as your male colleagues in the same job should be treated as standard procedure. Don't be shy about ensuring that if you're doing the same work as a man, you're paid the same as he is. This is an everyday action of speaking up that can make real change for you and others.

THE CONFIDENCE GAP

Confidence is another big issue. According to a Hewlett Packard report published in *Forbes* magazine in 2014, women will typically only apply for jobs if they match the job spec 100 per cent. In contrast men typically apply for jobs if they hold only 60 per cent of the required qualifications and skills.

THIS DIFFERENCE IS MASSIVE.

It means that women are significantly more likely to apply for lower-paid and lower-status jobs while men are more likely to pursue higher-paid, higher-status jobs, not because they will be better at those roles or they're more qualified. Oh no. It's simply because they are men and have the confidence to go for it, while women are more likely to play it safe.

Now, men are of course completely allowed to be ambitious and pursue their dreams! But women should feel just as able to follow their passions and aim high. Yet they don't. There are lots of reasons for this, and they all need combatting, but you can do something to help. You can speak up! The next time you apply for a job or an apprenticeship or college/uni place, don't underestimate yourself. Aim high. If you're not

100 per cent qualified for a job, go for it regardless. You are more than capable of learning on the job. You can get those top roles. You are just as worthy and capable as anyone else.

THE STATUS GAP

The gender pay gap and this huge confidence gap link with a third and wider gender gap: that of status. In 2016, *The Guardian* discovered that there are more CEOs working for the top FTSE 100 companies called John than there are female CEOs.

HOW RIDICULOUS IS THAT!

And it doesn't stop there. *The Guardian* also found that female leaders of these companies are outnumbered by Davids, Ians, Marks or Andrews by nearly five to one. In contrast they found that a grand total of SEVEN women run Britain's leading companies. Yep, just seven out of 100.

This isn't just a British problem. The *New York Times* found that significantly more men named John were running America's leading companies than women too. Furthermore, an Ernst & Young report found that for every woman on the board of American companies, there were 1.03 Jameses, Roberts, Johns and Williams. (What is the deal with the name John?!)

There's a whole heap of reasons why this may be – from institutional barriers to the mainstream discrimination against women in the workplace – but the overall problem is something YOU can help to tackle through everyday campaigning actions. Don't let any male-only boards of directors put you off reaching for the top of whichever career you choose to pursue.

YOU HAVE THE POWER TO CHANGE THESE FIGURES.

You can be the first CEO of any business if you want to be. The next generation of businesswomen could start with YOU.

GET READY, WORLD!

Whichever opportunities you explore, or avenues you take to make changes, know that you can do amazing things. There are currently gaps and barriers that differentiate the sexes, from the pay gap to the status gap, but you can change them. Like the women before us who spoke up to ensure we can go to university today, you too can make sure that the women of tomorrow face fewer struggles. You can ensure there are just as many women as men on our top business boards of the future. You can be those women on those boards. So much can be changed. These changes start with you.

YOUR NEXT STEPS

MORE SO THAN EVER BEFORE, YOU HAVE THE POWER TO CHANGE THE WORLD.

With the tips and tricks you've picked up throughout this book, and your own hard work and fierce determination, you can do anything. There is no problem too big or too small for you to solve. It might not be quick, but it's time for you to make your mark. It's time for you to join the barrier-smashing women of tomorrow and solve the problems we face today.

If you ever question why I'm talking to you, then answer me this:

IF YOU DON'T SPEAK UP, WHO WILL? NOW IS YOUR TIME.

You are qualified to change the world in so many ways.

YOU ARE GOING TO DO A BRILLIANT JOB.

Here are just a few reasons why you have the power to make changes to even age-old problems by using our toolkit:

First, you hold the power to change the world because you know exactly how to run your own campaign. You began to climb our five steps to instigating changes when you opened our **TOOLKIT** right at the beginning of this book. You conquered your first step by finding the specific issue that you want to tackle. Next, you identified your **DECISION MAKER(S)** and found out who exactly you need to direct your campaign towards. On Step Three you undertook your all-important campaign **RESEARCH** and discovered exactly what you need to do to make sure you WIN. On the penultimate step you selected the racing vehicles that will secure your success! You decided which campaigning **PLATFORMS** — whether that be a petition, letter, demonstration or utilizing social media — will support and suit your campaigning goal best. Having done all of this hard work, you heroically reached our fifth and final step: you prepared to **LAUNCH** your campaign!

All of this qualifies you to change the world, plain and simple. These steps and tips will always be here for you if you ever feel at all lost or in need of campaign reminders/advice.

WITH THESE YOU CAN DO
ANYTHING!

If somehow you're still not convinced that you are perfectly qualified to change the world then don't sweat, I have plenty more reasons for you!

You have also been trained in the **ART OF BOUNCING BACK.** You know exactly how to slay trolls and turn your failures into your strengths. These are vital for any modern-day warrior woman! With them you can always succeed and make a difference, no matter how many challenges you face in your campaign journey or in your everyday life.

As if that wasn't enough, you can use this book to not only **SPEAK UP** and instigate changes, but also to open up conversations about **RELATIONSHIPS, CONSENT, LOVE, FEMINISM AND BODY POSITIVITY.** You're armed not only with the guidance to make changes, but the information to **CHANGE NARRATIVES** and wider conversations about women as a whole.

THAT'S PRETTY KICK-ASS!

You've started to think about what your next steps are on the road to becoming an awesome activist.

You might choose your gladiator training ground to be at university, in an apprenticeship, or diving straight into the world of work. In these places you can hone your debating skills, practise everyday activism and join a union or run campaigns full-time or as a side hustle. All these options can lead you to pursue your goals and dreams of making a difference, whichever is your priority at this point in your life.

Finally, you are queen of speaking up because you know how to use all of these tips and tricks throughout your life. No matter what you decide to do, you can change anything. Whether you want to go to university, pursue an apprenticeship or training opportunity, dive straight into work, or something entirely different, you can always speak up to solve any problem you face. No matter what you decide to do, you'll forever be a badass campaigner, ready to change the world. Change starts with you, with your voice.

YOU HAVE POWER.

YOU HAVE CONFIDENCE.

You have the knowledge to make changes. To have graduated our campaigning crash course and delved into many tips for change-makers, you are hard-working, tenacious and focused. You can be a visionary. You can make the changes you want to see. You can be an ICON. This is your time. Online campaigning is a new game. It is yours to win. Now it's your turn:

SPEAK UP!

END TAMPON TAX TIMELINE!

APRIL 2014 My friend Verity sends me an article about the tax we pay on period products, including tampons and sanitary pads. I get angry.

MAY 2014 I launch the End Tampon Tax petition calling for an end to tampon tax. This same day I find out that while tampons and sanitary pads are deemed luxurious enough to be taxed, a bizarre cocktail of apparently more essential items escape tax altogether, including alcoholic sugar jellies, bingo and maintaining **PRIVATE HELICOPTERS!**

AUGUST 2014 The campaign earns its first national coverage. The *Telegraph* publishes a story about the campaign. While this brings our first wave of trolling, and dealing with this is difficult, our supporters and signatures grow exponentially. We soon reach 100,000 signatures! Despite trolls, our campaign is stronger than ever.

For the next year we write for lots of different publications, including the *Huffington Post* and the *Telegraph*, to raise awareness of our campaign. We do this by contacting them and pitching our article ideas. You can do this too!

Campaigners in Canada, led by superwoman Jill Piebiak, email us to say they are setting up their own tampon tax petition. Our first sister campaign is born! We start to see this is a worldwide problem, and not one tied specifically to the UK. Their hard work strengthens ours, and vice versa. From this point on more sister petitions start popping up across the world!

JANUARY 2015 Stella Creasy MP (who campaigned to end tampon tax when she was at uni) joins team End Tampon Tax. She is the first politician we meet with in Parliament. She introduces us to Dawn Primarolo MP (the woman behind the original campaign that lowered tampon tax from 17.5 per cent to 5 per cent in 2001) and we hash out plans to end the tax once and for all . . .

MARCH-MAY 2015 The 2015 general election is creeping up on us. During the election period, our End Tampon Tax campaign makes its way into EVERY SINGLE mainstream political manifesto. ALL parties, from Labour and the Conservatives, to the Green Party and the Liberal Democrats, announce their support for the axing of tampon tax. **THIS IS MAJOR!**

APRIL 2015 We reach 200,000 amazing, brilliant, heroic supporters! With this cohort of supporters on our side, we can REALLY make changes!

We hand our petition to Number 11 Downing Street. This marks our first contact with the Treasury's office. I organize a protest just outside of Parliament to mark this huge milestone! It is seriously nerve-wracking. It is the first protest I have ever been to – and I am organizing it! Nonetheless, HUNDREDS of supporters come to Whitehall to support us. **THIS IS EPiC**! It helps us to not only raise the profile of our campaign, but to tackle the period taboo too.

MAY 2015 Our sisters in Canada WIN! Canada votes to axe tampon tax. They become the first government in the world to do so since we started our petition **(WHOOP WHOOP!)**.

JUNE 2015 I graduate from uni and never have to revise again!

AUGUST 2015 Paula Sherriff MP joins team End Tampon Tax. We meet with her in Parliament to discuss our next campaigning moves. **SHE IS AWESOME!**

OCTOBER 2015 Paula Sherriff MP heroically proposes a motion to end tampon tax in Parliament. This is like a school debate, only involving ministers and politicians. Despite our best efforts to get this motion through Parliament, we fail. It is rejected by 305 to 287 votes. Parliament decide not to end tampon tax.

Despite this setback (and it is a big one!) it gains a LOT of media traction. Even Russell Howard dedicates a section of his Good News show in November to discussing: 'Why Cutting Tax Credit and Taxing Tampons is BULL$#!T'. Our campaign ends up growing in strength!

NOVEMBER 2015 George Osborne, then Chancellor of the Exchequer, responds to our campaign for the first time ever. He deals with the pressure that the loss of Paula Sherriff's amendment caused one month ago in an AMAZING way: he launches the world's first Tampon Tax Fund and in doing so becomes the first chancellor to say the word 'tampon' in Parliament EVER!!

This fund gives £15m (the annual revenue generated from tampon tax) to female-focused charities each year. It continues to do so today! LOTS of charities have benefited from this, including the amazing Eve Appeal, which raises awareness and research of all five gynae cancers.

DECEMBER 2015 OUR FRENCH SISTER PETITION WINS!
France votes in favour of reducing the tampon tax. It is cut from 20 per cent to 5 per cent.

JANUARY 2016 Barack Obama, then President of the USA, announces his support for the End Tampon Tax campaign, which is making waves across America thanks to our sisters stateside, in an interview with YouTube superstar Ingrid Nilsen. *heart eyes*

Following Barack Obama's AWESOME support, **WE REACH 300,000 SIGNATURES!!!!**

FEBRUARY 2016 Superdrug becomes the first brand to join team End Tampon Tax! They begin a scheme to give customers back their tampon tax through store points whenever they purchase period products, period!

EU referendum is announced. This puts pressure on our political leaders to either prove or disprove that the EU is a modern and progressive body that we should/n't continue to be a member of. This impacts lots of campaigns, including ours.

MARCH 2016 David Cameron, then prime minister of the UK, joins team End Tampon Tax!! He proposes a tampon-tax-ending motion to the EU, the body that holds ultimate taxation power over all member states (in 2016 this includes the UK). This proposal is unlike any other made in history. It is the FIRST to attempt to allow all member states to lower their tax on any single good. It makes history.

WE HIT NATIONAL NEWS FOR THE FIRST TIME! We are asked to join a load of news shows, including Channel 5 News, ITV News, BBC Victoria Derbyshire, to talk about the imminent end to tampon tax.

David Cameron's motion PASSES with the UNANIMOUS support of all 28 member countries. This means that the UK could finally end tampon tax! OUR CAMPAIGN WINS! We win the political battle against tampon tax!

MAY 2016 We believe tampon tax will officially end. But It doesn't! Implementing the end of tampon tax is taking longer than we ever expected. This begins our waiting game . . .

211

Jeremy Corbyn, leader of the Labour Party, announces his support for team End Tampon Tax in Parliament during a debate on the matter. Pressure mounts for David Cameron and George Osborne to implement the axing of tampon tax.

We organize our second protest outside Westminster to put even more pressure on Parliament to implement the changes they have secured. SO many of our amazing supporters join us (FYI, my mama joined in a super-stylish red-spotted tampon-tax-inspired coat, which is EVERYTHING). Even our sisters from the USA, led by superwoman Jennifer Weiss-Wolf, come over to support us.

JUNE 2016 Molly Scott Cato MEP joins team End Tampon Tax! She organizes a conference in the European parliament called 'Taxation Is a Feminist Policy' to show that the EU supports those member states who want to lower their tax rates on period products. She invites me to speak at her conference in front of the European parliament! **THIS IS EPIC!**

JULY 2016 The *Guardian* and Nesta name me one of their top Radical Thinkers of 2016!

NOVEMBER 2016 We launch sister petitions to help end period poverty. These lobby major period product producer Procter & Gamble to donate period products to homeless shelters. **WE REACH 45,000 SIGNATURES IN JUST 24 HOURS!** This Homeless Period project launches to show the government that, while we wait for the tampon-tax-ending piece of legislation to be technically enacted, we're keeping an eye on all things period! We are dedicated to making further changes until tampon tax completely ends.

NEW Chancellor of the Exchequer Philip Hammond MP follows in George Osborne's footsteps by mentioning the word 'tampon' again! He announces in his Autumn Statement that the Tampon Tax Fund will continue, as he gives another £15m to female-focused charities. In doing so he also reminds us that tampon tax will be axed as soon as it's legally possible to do so. He does so with the seal of approval from new Prime Minister, Theresa May!

DECEMBER 2016 BBC includes the End Tampon Tax campaign in its 100 Women Series! We appear on BBC World News for the first time EVER!

Channel 4 News joins team End Tampon Tax by airing national coverage of both the End Tampon Tax campaign and our Homeless Period project.

213

JANUARY 2017 Radio 4's Woman's Hour supports our projects by discussing period poverty and tampon tax!

We appear on BBC One's *The Big Questions* to talk about the amazing ways the internet can empower women.

FEBRUARY 2017 Both BBC Three and Oxford University offer their support for team End Tampon Tax! While BBC Three air a special clip raising awareness of both the period taboo and period poverty, Oxford University holds the first UK conference to discuss these topics since we started campaigning! We're also invited to BBC Radio 5 Live to talk about these problems.

MARCH 2017 I write for the *Guardian* to celebrate International Women's Day and raise awareness of period poverty.

Charity Freedom4Girls publishes a study that shows 10 per cent of UK schoolgirls are missing school because of period poverty. Our schoolgirl sister campaigns (including Amika George's End Period Poverty petition) launch in response to this, which lobby for free period products in schools!

Philip Hammond MP announces more money will fund female-focused charities via the Tampon Tax Fund in his Spring Statement!

APRIL 2017 UK prime minister Theresa May calls a UK general election.

APRIL-JUNE 2017 ALL major political parties feature period poverty and say they support axing tampon tax as soon as it's legally possible in their manifestos.

SEPTEMBER 2017 The Labour Party announces its national policy to end period poverty, pressuring the Conservatives to do the same.

I get into Oxford University to study my Masters in Women's Studies and hope this will help me to campaign! But I also have to revise again. (BOO!)

OCTOBER 2017 Bodyform launches a new advert involving RED liquid instead of weird blue liquid (what was that even about, anyway?!) to represent period blood for the FIRST TIME EVER in UK advertising history. In doing so they smash the period taboo.

Oh, and they join our campaign to help end period poverty by promising to donate 200,000 packs of period products to vulnerable women and homeless shelters.

The Tampon Tax Fund awards an anti-abortion charity £250,000, despite opposition from campaigners. This causes HUGE controversy. Supporters begin to think that the End Tampon Tax campaign is anti-abortion, despite the fact that the government selects the Fund's recipients, and not us. We are powerless in this situation. I definitely feel this failure. But we work on proposals to make sure controversial charities are not awarded funding generated from tampon tax in the future. From that point on, the responsibility of awarding funds is distributed to a number of smaller charities and authorities who have since worked hard to avoid upsetting people who menstruate, who are, for the moment, forced to pay into this fund.

NOVEMBER 2017 BBC News launch a tampon tax calculator to help people find out just how much they have spent on the tax!

DECEMBER 2017 MAJOR protest called the 'pink protest' happens in Westminster to raise awareness of period poverty and tampon tax. **THOUSANDS OF PEOPLE ARE THERE IN SUPPORT!**

JANUARY 2018 California axes tampon tax! Our sisters in California WIN!

Philip Hammond MP announces that tampon tax might still technically be here until 2022, as legislation is held up AGAIN following Brexit.

MARCH 2018 For the third year in a row the Tampon Tax Fund is announced! £15m goes to female-focused charities once again.

JUNE 2018 I graduate from Oxford and seriously will never have to revise again. **MUHAHA!**

JULY 2018 India axes tampon tax! Our sisters across India WIN!

AUGUST 2018 Scottish government announces a new £5.2m period poverty scheme to ensure ALL students across Scotland receive FREE period products. This arms every school, college and university student in the country with tampons and sanitary pads, which the government say is aimed at 'banishing the scourge of period poverty' among pupils.

THAT'S PRETTY KICK-ASS!

SEPTEMBER 2018 Australia axes tampon tax. Our sisters in Australia WIN!

OCTOBER 2018 Spain reduces their tampon tax from 10 per cent to 4 per cent.

NOVEMBER 2018 Nevada becomes the tenth US state to end tampon tax.

So where are we today? Well, we are STILL waiting for the tampon-tax-ending legislation that David Cameron approved and committed the UK government to way back in May 2016, to go through both the EU and the UK parliament. These pieces of legislation have already been confirmed. We won our campaign when the government committed to ending tampon tax back in May 2016. They cannot go back on that.

TAMPON TAX WILL END.

It's just a case of waiting for tampon-tax-ending legislation to go through the necessary processes to make them law. It's a frustrating period (pun intended) but it's worth the wait. In the meantime, we need as many people to speak up about issues like tampon tax. We need to continue to make noise until tampon tax can technically end.

THIS IS MY CAMPAIGN TIMELINE. WHAT WILL YOURS LOOK LIKE?

INDEX

ONLINE RESOURCES

DEALING WITH TROLLS

The BBC have created an interactive 'How Do I Deal With Internet Trolls?' page:
www.bbc.co.uk/guides/zcq72p3#zqpnsg8

change.org have created a list of tips for dealing with trolls:
www.change.org/l/uk/tackling-the-trolls-safer-internet-day-2017
Childnet is a charity making the internet safer for young people:
www.childnet.com

SEX AND RELATIONSHIPS

Brook is an online advice and support for all aspects of sex and relationships:
www.brook.org.uk

SEXUAL ASSAULT

Childline provides counselling services for young people affected by sexual abuse:
www.childline.org.uk / 0800 1111

The NSPCC provides support for young people who have been affected by sexual abuse:
www.nspcc.org.uk / 0808 800 5000

Papyrus is a helpline for young people dealing with suicide, depression or emotional distress:
www.papyrus-uk.org / 0800 068 4141

ACKNOWLEDGEMENTS

A HUGE thank you to all the schoolgirls who have spoken to me about campaigning over the years. Your enthusiasm for making changes and influencing decision makers has made me so excited for the future. And to every single person who backed the End Tampon Tax campaign, including Verity who inspired the whole project, the superwomen at change.org, and each and everyone who signed the petition, you are amazing. Every supporter has taught me that girls and women hold SO much power when they speak up and use our superpower, the internet. You have made huge changes and have inspired this book.

To Chloe Seager, my fantastic literary agent, who made my dreams to write a book that supports girls absolutely come true. To Rebecca Lewis-Oakes, my amazing editor, you embody completely what this book is all about. You have kept me laughing (sometimes to the point of tears) while writing this book. To Emma Dods and the team at Egmont, including the wonderful design team, who believed so encouragingly in this project.

To all of the wonderful women who gave me quotes, advice and their time for this book, including Helen Pankhurst, Charlie Graggs, Jennifer Weiss-Wolf, Frances Scott, Kajal Odedra and the AMAZING change.org team.

To my dearest friends who have always supported me and given me so much advice for writing since I left school, including Adam, Ollie, Vik, Sarah, Paul, Emma, Laura, Gussie (who proofread so many of these chapters!), Hannah, Danielle, Artie, James and Ellie.

Thank you to Brook for their advice and support on Chapters 3 and 4, and to the Career Development Institute for their advice on Chapter 5.

Finally to my family, without whom this book would not have been possible. Thank you for spending countless hours proofreading, listening to me read through these chapters and talk about them relentlessly. In particular to my parents, Tracy and Demitri, for letting me move back home to Portugal, and steal all of your iced tea supplies in the meantime, to write this book. And to my twin Julia (who actually is a black-belt/ninja in real life) for inspiring my ninja obsession and showing me the power of women who work together. To my lovely cousins and super granny, and to my grandpa who always encouraged and believed in us but sadly passed away a few weeks before I finished writing this book.

I hope that this book, which in itself is a product of all of the help and support I am so lucky to have, can support you, a badass who can make a massive difference.

WOMEN CAN CHANGE

THE WORLD.

IT ALL BEGINS NOW.

IT ALL STARTS WITH YOU!